THE FOREIGN POLICY
OF THE POWERS

THE FOREIGN POLICY OF THE POWERS

FRANCE, GERMANY, GREAT BRITAIN, ITALY, JAPAN, SOVIET RUSSIA, THE UNITED STATES

By

Jules Cambon
Richard von Kühlmann
Sir Austen Chamberlain
Dino Grandi
Viscount Ishii
Karl Radek
John W. Davis

With an Introduction by
Hamilton Fish Armstrong

Essay Index Reprint Series

BOOKS FOR LIBRARIES PRESS
FREEPORT, NEW YORK

First Published 1935 for Council on Foreign Relations, Inc.
Reprinted 1970

INTERNATIONAL STANDARD BOOK NUMBER:
0-8369-1804-5

LIBRARY OF CONGRESS CATALOG CARD NUMBER:
77-111831

PRINTED IN THE UNITED STATES OF AMERICA

CONTENTS

THE FOREIGN POLICY OF THE POWERS

INTRODUCTION 1
    BY HAMILTON FISH ARMSTRONG
    Editor of "Foreign Affairs"

I. FRANCE 3
    BY JULES CAMBON
    Former Ambassador to Germany

II. GERMANY 25
    BY RICHARD VON KÜHLMANN
    Former Secretary of State for Foreign Affairs

III. GREAT BRITAIN 54
    BY SIR AUSTEN CHAMBERLAIN
    Former Secretary of State for Foreign Affairs

IV. ITALY 78
    BY DINO GRANDI
    Ambassador to Great Britain

V. JAPAN 102
    BY VISCOUNT ISHII
    Former Minister for Foreign Affairs

VI. SOVIET RUSSIA 119
    BY KARL RADEK
    Editor of "Izvestia"

VII. THE UNITED STATES 143
    BY JOHN W. DAVIS
    Former Ambassador to Great Britain

INTRODUCTION

THIRTY years ago Hugo Münsterberg thought it likely that the "climatic equilibrium" of the United States, upset by the extension of American influence into the tropics through the acquisition of the Philippine Islands, would eventually be restored by another extension into the Canadian northwest.[1] He probably was over-impressed by the uncompromising tone being taken by American officials and press in the Alaska boundary dispute at the time he was writing his book. At any rate, his diagnosis proved incorrect. Today, Americans do not crave a square inch of Canadian soil by conquest or as a gift. The universal feeling is that we already have plenty of space, plenty of people and plenty of problems of our own.

So strong is this feeling, and so strong the desire to avoid risks of foreign entanglement and war where no vital national interests are concerned, that the United States Government has been prompted to reduce its responsibilities in many directions. A date has been set for our withdrawal from the Philippines; there has been a cessation of intervention in the affairs of Nicaragua and Haiti; and a new interpretation of the meaning of Cuban independence has been given by the abrogation of the Platt Amendment. Our definite policy, in other words, is to slough off responsibilities outside the North American continent and reverse what in 1904, and for some time thereafter, seemed the instinctive and natural growth of American imperialism. And on the continent itself the attitude of "good neighbor" toward Canada and Mexico has become accepted so much as a matter of course by the American public that a suggestion like the one made by Professor Münsterberg

[1] "The Americans," p. 216 (1904).

a generation ago only awakens a smile and the reflection that it is a risky business to try to describe a "national will", or to foretell a people's destiny even when it seems most "manifest."

We none the less see that there are racial characteristics and conditions set by climate and geography which from generation to generation continue to influence a people's hopes and fears as well as the methods its leaders use to fulfill the one and mitigate the other. The passage of time and the achievements of man's inventive genius modify those traits and alter those conditions. But enough underlying trends exist to make it profitable for us to search them out and attempt to relate them to present events and to policies now shaping for the future.

That was the task set the eminent statesmen and diplomats whose essays compose the present volume. Here and there some of them may seem to have emphasized the logic and necessity of certain policies of the moment instead of holding rigorously to a consideration of the main theme—namely, how far national policy, despite zigzags and ups-and-downs, conforms to a pattern dictated not by personal inspiration or sudden manœuvre but by continuing material and psychological factors. The reader will be quick to detect any such attempts to interchange cause and effect, to put wish for fulfillment, and will take account of the difficulty of attaining complete objectivity in discussing a question so beset with difficulties.

These papers appeared originally in *Foreign Affairs*. They were planned as a connected series, and it is hoped that the aim of their authors will be served by bringing them together now in one place. In a world where standards and traditions are shifting with confusing rapidity it is a relief to be told that some guide-posts still stand, and useful to know what they are.

HAMILTON FISH ARMSTRONG.

CHAPTER I

FRANCE

By Jules Cambon

AIMLESS and contradictory as appear the happenings in the history of each nation, we nevertheless are able to discern, when we survey them as a whole and in their proper sequence, that they are not disobedient to certain laws. Revolutions do not work any definite change; the institutions which a people set up are only the expression of its ideas at a certain moment, and they do not modify its position with regard to other nations. The relations of a government with foreign governments may be affected, but not the necessities imposed upon it by its geographical position, its history, its need to live. That is what we call its traditions. At the present moment, we have a striking example of this fact. The policy of the Soviet Government in the Far East may differ in method from that which the Tsarist Government followed; but it does not differ from it in spirit or in objective.

The geographical position of a nation, indeed, is the principal factor conditioning its foreign policy—the principal reason why it must have a foreign policy at all. This is a truism of which the whole history of England is a demonstration. English history is determined and limited by the fact that Great Britain is an island. She is a European Power, but as she is separated from the Continent by the sea she has not experienced the constant tribulations of the Continental states. Twice, in the times of Philip II and of Napoleon I, she has feared attacks on her own territory; but the history of those events showed how impossible it was for her adversaries to penetrate her natural defenses. Hence her disdain for the military establishments of the Continent, and her inbred dislike of the system of conscription. Oftentimes she has mixed in European quarrels, but only to play the rôle of an umpire who is unwilling for the victor to be too victorious. And when the time came to make peace it has not been hard to sense that she did not consider her own security as being in the least at stake. Elizabeth and Cromwell, Pitt and Palmerston, had the same views, which one may characterize as "insular" in the real sense of the word.

On the other hand, England's naval policy has had quite a different character, because it was essential that she should never encounter any superior sea power. All the other nations have had to struggle against her for the freedom of the seas. Her maritime imperialism grew out of her need of assuring her security and her sources of supply. One can even say that changes perceptible recently in certain sections of British opinion prove the truth of the above observation regarding England's traditional policy. Certainly the agitation in favor of an increase in the British air force is the reflex of the development of Germany's power in the air. Not being able to rely for defense against air attack on the fact that she is an island, England is seeking to increase her powers of resistance, and to that extent is abandoning her tradition of relying solely upon her navy.

And cannot what I have said of England also be said of the United States of America? Separated from the Old Worlds by two oceans, her only neighbors too weak to dare to contradict her, free from any fears regarding security, possessing in her immense territory all the riches of the earth, all the forces and products of industry, America has almost limitless liberty of action. That is why expressions of the noble idealism which is the real honor of the American spirit sometimes sound strange in the ears of the European nations, brought up as they have been in other circumstances and preoccupied with hopes and fears in which the United States has no share. The geographical isolation of the American people has given it its force, has allowed it to become great and powerful. The Monroe Doctrine is nothing but the expression of its determination to let nothing impair that isolation. This celebrated doctrine has been the cornerstone of the American Government's policy for a century, and today it explains why the United States has not wished to participate in the League of Nations.

France, like England, has sought through the centuries to realize her destiny; but, like England, which by reason of her special situation has put her trust in a preponderant naval power, France, whose frontiers to the north and to the east were open to invasion, has put her trust in military power. And so these two Powers, whose behavior at first glance seems to have been so different, in reality obey the same instinct: both look for security, each in the manner dictated by its geographical position.

It is true that sometimes accidental happenings have misled or bewildered foreign opinion as to the real objectives of England and France. But we do not understand history if we do not give the right value to accidents, as well as to the personal schemes of those who play great historical rôles at particular moments. I should like to cite two examples from the history of France.

France is often accused of imperialism because throughout her history she has wished to make the Rhine her frontier. The origin of this tendency, which goes far back, must be made clear. Caesar in his "Commentaries," Tacitus in his "Customs of the Germans," Strabo himself, fixed the Rhine as the boundary of Gaul; the jurists who played so important a part in the policy of the ancient kings and who loved to rely on old texts to justify their territorial claims, never failed to cite these hoary traditions, which gradually became part of the national soul. When, during the wars of the French Revolution, the armies of the Republic entered into the Rhenish provinces, they certainly believed that they were taking possession again of what had always belonged to them. And our long occupation of those lands left a deep imprint on the Rhenish people themselves. The Foreign Minister of the German Empire, Kiderlen-Waechter, one day admitted to me that up to 1866 France would have been able to reëstablish the Rhine frontier without encountering any opposition from the local population. It was the foundation of the new Germany, he said, which had changed this state of mind.

Napoleon and his prodigious conquests intoxicated France. In spite of that, and glorious as his achievement was, it is not paradoxical to say that this epoch in our history was an "accident." At St. Helena he avowed that he had wanted to set up a great Germany and a great Italy, to join in a single mass all the peoples of the same race. He foresaw the future. But the very grandiosity of his views proved how foreign his genius was to the traditional policy of France, who always regarded herself as the guardian of weak princes. Napoleon's imperial spirit, founded on the memories of the grandeur that was Rome, was not hampered by a consideration of French interests *per se*. His gaze went beyond our frontiers. But the tradition of our policy was something altogether different; it cared only for France; it was essentially conservative, circumspect, deliberate. That is what Rivarol indicated very well when in 1783, in his celebrated essay on the universality of the French language, he wrote: "France acts against her best interests and misunderstands her rôle when she lends herself to the spirit of conquest." And Vergennes, the great Minister of Louis XVI, said in 1777, in his report to the King: "France must fear expansion much more than desire it." These principles were merely the practical application of the ideas of Montesquieu, who in his "Spirit of Laws" invited sovereigns always to have a wary eye open to the inconveniences, not to say the dangers, of grandeur.

In the eighteenth century, then, the policy of France, as defined by her philosophers and her statesmen, was far from being imperialistic. It based itself rather upon the idea of the balance of power. It seemed as though the peace of Europe and the security of each of its component parts would necessarily result from an equilibrium. Here is the explanation of the sudden transformation of French policy in the eighteenth century, sometimes called the overthrow of the alliances. France had supported Prussia in her early stages and had aided her to become strong. When Frederick II openly menaced the established order in Germany, the government at Versailles ranged itself on the side of Austria and Maria Theresa. French opinion received this abandonment of the Russian alliance with every sign of mistrust; but it undoubtedly was in conformity with the policy of the balance of power followed by M. de Choiseul.

For the rest, we must admit that at the start this

policy of equilibrium was of a purely empirical character and grew out of events. Later on, naturally enough, theorists were found to give it its name and to make of it the fundamental law on which rested peace between the European Powers.

Today, after the war of 1914, people jeer at the guarantee of peace afforded by the old system of the balance of power. It is described as an illusion. That is going too far, but we must recognize that democracy does not rest content with quantitative analyses of opposing forces, carried on quietly in diplomatic offices. It demands new methods which will permit weak nations, like the strong, to play a rôle in the settlement of matters of general concern. This is a step forward; the League of Nations is constantly taking on more importance and authority, and assuredly is destined to develop further still. But all that does not make it any less prudent always to maintain a certain balance between the Powers. What is happening today in the case of naval disarmament is evidence of what I say. The United States and Great Britain seek to adjust their naval armaments, but the condition which they set to any action is that it shall not impair naval parity between them. To each the idea that it might wake up one day to find itself in the presence of a superior naval force is intolerable.

It is useful, then, to search the past and learn why and how the system of the balance of power came into being, and to follow through successive centuries the application which has been made of it. Perhaps I shall be pardoned an historical digression. It will allow us —in spite of momentary accidents which now and then break the sequence—to recognize the unity of purpose which has characterized French policy in dealing with the difficulties which have always faced it. So we shall be led to understand what are its permanent characteristics.

We must go back to the end of the Middle Ages to find the origins of French foreign policy in modern times. The Hundred Years' War between France and England, which marked the end of this formative period, at first had the characteristics of a feudal war, but even in the midst of their miseries the French people developed a common consciousness. Jeanne d'Arc personified the dawn of national feeling, and that is why she appears to us the greatest figure in our history. It was not long afterwards, at the time of the Renaissance, that the French people, having at last constituted themselves into a nation, found that they were encircled on all sides—south, east and north—by a single sovereign power. The House of Austria ruled Germany, the Low Countries, Spain. The Emperor Charles V was the most powerful potentate that the world had known since Charlemagne, and the common saying was that the sun never set on his dominions. He had genius, ambition and prodigious activity, and immense forces under his control. Inevitably he wished to stifle the independence of France, which, placed in the center of his possessions, prevented him from unifying them. Nature itself had made Francis I, who reigned at Paris, his rival and his enemy. Poets and writers of romance have been pleased to paint Francis I merely as a lover of the arts and of pleasure. They have not seen in him the politician that he was. He was unlucky in war, but he was the initiator of a policy which his successors had to follow, a policy which triumphed in the eighteenth century and which since then has been followed through many changing circumstances —I dare to say it—down to the present day.

Note that from the very beginning this policy, which was to unite all the French, was disturbed and endangered by the passions which divided Frenchmen amongst themselves. Religious wars rent the country for nearly a century and brought the Spaniards to Paris itself. Two tendencies have always existed in France and have thrown her statesmen into two camps. Those who in the sixteenth century had a liberal and aristocratic spirit and tended toward reform were partisans of union with England. Admiral Coligny, who represented this party, maintained relations with Queen Elizabeth. On the contrary, those who belonged to the Catholic party, the Guises and the chiefs of the League, wished to rely on Spain and Germany. Between the two, the King and his policies manœuvred as best they could. It sometimes seems as though even in our day these two tendencies still exist and continue to set Frenchmen against each other.

Be that as it may, the nature of things led the Monarchy to seek allies against the might of the German Emperor. In this way she became the supporter of the weak German princes who were trying to escape the talons of the imperial eagle, and who for the most part became partisans of the Reformation. Hence the rôle of France in the Thirty Years' War. And hence the policy of France always to be the ally of the little Powers of Europe. It was this same search for an equilibrium which led Francis I to court the friendship of the Grand Turk (to the great scandal of Christendom), which had for its consequence the opening up of the East to Christian traders of all nationalities.

Our great Henry IV was one of the first to inaugurate the policy of coöperating with the weak and of showing moderation in spite of strength. His favorite minister, Sully, defined it when he wrote in one of his reports: "The Kings of France should aim to acquire friends, allies and confederates, bound by the sure ties of commerce and common interests, rather than to nourish ambitious projects and thus draw irreconcilable hatreds down upon their heads."

Princes of the Church though they were, both Richelieu and Mazarin backed the Protestant princes of Germany against the Emperor. Mazarin even went so far as to form an alliance with Cromwell. The steady pursuit of this policy resulted in the Treaty of Westphalia which, through the Rhine League, secured the independence of the Protestant princes and gave Germany a constitution that lasted two centuries. This policy of alliances and compromises constituted what has been known as the classic system of French diplomacy. It corresponded to the national temperament, which mistrusts imagination in matters of state. The men responsible for this policy were not theorists who stuck to their preconceptions regardless of hard facts; Jean-Jacques Rousseau and his disciples had not yet been born; and as our eminent historian, Albert Sorel, observes, "these great men had method without having any spirit of system."

Europe relied upon the balance of power, but when Louis XIV, abandoning the policy of moderation which France had followed until his time, appeared on the point of shattering it, he found aligned against him a coalition which included even our old allies. He has been reproached by many historians for accepting the inheritance of Charles II and thus entering upon the disastrous war of the Spanish Succession. However, he had serious reasons for acting as he did. If his grandson, the Duke of Anjou, had not ascended the throne of Spain, it would have passed into the hands of an Austrian Archduke, and once again France would have been faced with a united Spain and Austria, a combination which she had fought against for centuries. The war ended in a compromise. France no longer threatened Europe. By renouncing for himself and his descendants the right to reign in Paris, a Bourbon was permitted to reign in Madrid.

In my opinion, the worst result of Louis XIV's abandonment of our traditional policy was the distrust which it aroused towards us abroad. Perhaps we even suffer from it today.

Throughout the eighteenth century the policy of every European government was one of intrigue and ambition: the period is well represented by the skeptical and realistic Frederick II, who knew how to exploit the jealousies of the various courts. In France, statecraft completely lacked continuity. Louis XV, intelligent and weak, was typical of his epoch. He followed a policy separate and distinct from that of his ministers—what was called "le secret du Roi"—with results easy to imagine. By the time the Seven Years' War was over, France had lost all influence and authority. This became obvious when Prussia, Austria and Russia started to dismember Poland, and France found herself in no position to oppose them. The eclipse of French prestige was a tragedy for the little nations.

France learned her lesson. Vergennes, to whom Louis XVI intrusted the portfolio of foreign affairs, was imbued with the traditional ideals of the old régime, the ideals in particular of Henry IV and of Richelieu. His policy was one of moderation, of collaboration with the lesser Powers and support of the weak. Public opinion, piqued by the decline of national prestige under his predecessors, backed him up when he offered French military, financial and moral support to the United States, who wished to become an independent nation. In this he was but repeating the assistance given by France early in the seventeenth century to Portugal and the Low Countries.

Meanwhile the German Emperor, Joseph II, an ambitious and restless sovereign, wished to follow in the footsteps of Frederick II. Thinking to profit by his sister Marie Antoinette's influence at Versailles, he dreamed great dreams; he dreamed of annexing Bavaria to Austria, of creating a kingdom for the Elector of Bavaria in the Netherlands, and of buying French complicity by ceding part of Belgium to her. He even went so far as to offer us Luxemburg. Vergennes spurned these proposals; in fact he urged the German princes (who were of course much disturbed) to unite against the Emperor, and in a memorandum on this subject prepared for the King he wrote: "If one stops to consider the crying injustice which would be entailed by the acceptance of the idea of partitioning the Netherlands, no honest man can contemplate it seriously." And the Ambassador, Baron de Breteuil, said: "The King should look upon himself as guardian of the lesser princes. This policy has for centuries constituted the glory and security of the Crown." These statesmen, in other words, based the country's security upon the principle of respecting the rights of others and they did not separate the peace of France from that of Europe.

Such were the ideas, also, of two men destined one

day to play an important rôle at the start of the Revolution, Mirabeau and Talleyrand. Both were partisans of the English alliance and hated the spirit of conquest. Territorial bargainings between states, wrote Mirabeau in his book on the Prussian Monarchy, are iniquitous, and added: "It is arbitrary and tyrannous to make such exchanges without consulting the inhabitants."

"Consulting the inhabitants"—these are new words and new ideas in international relations. Despite the storm of revolution, despite the Napoleonic wars, despite the reaction of the Holy Alliance, they persisted and little by little made their way. They reappeared in the nineteenth century, and they furnish the main clue to an understanding of its events.

But the Revolution, which at first had made much of its renunciation of the spirit of war and conquest, was to be swept along by its enemies into a war lasting for almost twenty-five years. The European courts were on the whole quite indifferent to the fate of the unfortunate Louis XVI; indeed, they congratulated one another upon the weakened and distracted state of France, and, profiting by a situation which left them with free hands, made haste to finish off what remained of Poland amongst themselves. Nevertheless, a certain sense of the community of royal interests held them from going too far and led them to combat the Revolution as such. Brunswick made his pronouncement. But he had not counted upon what the enthusiasm of a people can do. Twenty-three years later the war ended at Waterloo with the defeat of Napoleon, but the ideas which his army had sowed across Europe were to germinate during the course of the nineteenth century. The Emperor had indeed been vanquished, but the Revolution triumphed.

I have already noted how the imagination of Napoleon, who when a young man in Egypt had dreamed like Alexander of eastern conquests, broke through all the traditional limits of French policy. According to Montesquieu, France is in the happy position of having a territory proportionate to her strength and abilities. This was also the opinion of Frenchmen of the eighteenth century, and particularly of Mirabeau's old friend Talleyrand, who used to say that real richness is to be won not by invading the territory of others, but by exploiting one's own to the utmost. He felt Europe's growing fear of the Emperor's insatiable ambition and he dreaded the future consequences of this ambition for France. He realized the dangerous fragility of the imperial edifice, and detached himself from the Napoleonic cause. His conceptions were those of the old school of French diplomacy; they could not be harnessed up with the grandiose schemes of the hero whose servant he had been. And when Napoleon had fallen, and Louis XVIII sent Talleyrand in 1814 to the Congress of Vienna, he drafted his own instructions so that they should carefully point out the need for France to inspire those around her with her spirit of moderation and her desire to be of service by aiding the cause of justice.

At Vienna, Talleyrand faced Europe's natural reaction against all the works of the Empire. Greedy ambitions demanded satisfaction on all sides. Prussia in particular gave herself over to the same spirit of conquest which had caused her so much suffering; in Germany, she hoped to aggrandize herself at the expense of the King of Saxony, who had long been the ally of Napoleon, and in France to seize our eastern provinces, which had formed part of the territory of the old Monarchy. Basing his claim on the principle of legitimacy, Talleyrand set himself to obtain the reestablishment of the pre-Revolutionary territorial status, including of course the maintenance of our old frontiers. He returned to the old doctrines of our diplomacy, and undertook the defense of the lesser states against Prussia. He managed to secure the support of England, and even of Austria, whom the Russian spectre was beginning to alarm. He triumphed, and with him triumphed the essential factor in French diplomacy which I have several times described. These negotiations at Vienna may be considered Talleyrand's diplomatic *chef-d'œuvre*. It was based on a principle which is of course open to discussion, that of legitimacy, and it thus introduced into the settlement of diplomatic problems the consideration of abstract ideas in a disinterested way and above the passions of the moment.

Fifteen years later, in 1830, the Belgian people rose against Holland, to whom they had been arbitrarily united in 1815. France was faithful to her past; she intervened to assist them to gain their independence, and her army took Antwerp. But though she thus was responsible for the triumph of liberty, she proved that she wished to draw no special profits from it, for when the Belgians offered the crown of Belgium to the Duke de Nemours, son of Louis Philippe, the King refused it. In consequence of this refusal Prince Leopold of Coburg became King of the Belgians.

This policy of restraint was so thoroughly a national policy, without distinction of party, that when on February 24, 1848, France proclaimed herself a Republic and Europe was being rocked to its foundations by the storm of revolution, the head of the provisional government, M. de Lamartine, sent to our agents abroad a celebrated circular in which he reaffirmed the conservative intentions of the Paris cabinet. This declaration meant much, because since the fall of Napoleon the slogan of the advanced parties of Europe had been the destruction of the European order as constituted by the Congress of Vienna.

When the republican régime was overthrown in its turn, the Emperor Napoleon III, fired by his uncle's example, dreamed of remaking Europe. Nevertheless, when he joined England in defense of Turkey against the Emperor Nicholas of Russia, his action was in accord with the precepts of the old Monarchy. In the same spirit at the Congress of Paris he undertook to establish the independence of Rumania, up to that time a mere Turkish province. The wave of democracy then sweeping Europe found in him a convinced supporter. He upheld Piedmont against Austria, and one may say without exaggeration that his benevolent attitude toward the states of the peninsula made him the chief author of Italian unity. But many who had applauded him for assisting the weak against the strong began to be troubled when it appeared that he was dominated by the Napoleonic rather than the old French tradition, and that national security was no longer his principal aim. The war of 1866 between Austria and Prussia justified these anxieties; the Europe of the Treaties of Westphalia and Vienna vanished. Public opinion in France was bewildered. The war of 1870 put the finishing touch to what had been begun in 1866. It marked the end of that balance of power which, under the leadership of France, had guaranteed some sort of order in Europe during two centuries.

In France, however, the Republic had succeeded the Empire. For forty-four years it acted wisely and prudently. France came to enjoy the esteem and friendship of all the Powers which were harassed by the presumptuous policies of Berlin.

Never before had the supreme objectives of a long line of our greatest statesmen imposed themselves so insistently upon France. We sought—we sought *only*

—security. I remember how once, while I was Ambassador at Berlin, a high German official suggested to me in the course of a private conversation that Germany, France and England might agree among themselves to divide up the Belgian Congo. I promptly repelled the suggestion, basing my position on our policy of always upholding the smaller states. In this I simply conformed with the *dicta* of Vergennes, Mirabeau and Talleyrand; and the ideas which led my German colleague to speak as he did were those of Frederick II, Hardenberg and Bismarck.

After the World War, at the Peace Conference of 1919, France naturally became the protagonist of all the nationalities which had been suppressed in centuries past; they wished to live again, and they invoked the principles of justice and liberty which had been avowed by the Allies throughout the long struggle. Poland came to life. The Czechs of Bohemia, who since the time of John Hus had often revolted against the Austrian domination, formed a young republic. Rumania won back her kinsmen in Transylvania. The Slavs of Croatia and of Illyria united with the Serbs of old Serbia to form Jugoslavia. And the French Republic gave these young nationalities the support which the old Monarchy, from Henry IV to Louis XVI, had given all nationalities who wished to live an independent life.

Democracy, dominant in the world at last, was unwilling to limit itself to the ordinary methods of the old diplomacy. And when President Wilson took the initiative in proposing that a League of Nations be set up he was merely responding to the obvious need for the creation of some new international instrument. Despite scoffs and misgivings, the League of Nations was established; its authority has grown; and it has become the most efficient instrument yet found for preventing international disputes from degenerating into armed conflicts. France's rôle at Geneva has been in keeping with her tradition. She is happy to see the lesser states granted a hearing on world problems on an equality with the Great Powers, for in this she sees the endorsement of her age-long policy towards them.

M. Briand, who has been active at Geneva and who put forward the anti-war proposal which has since become the Briand-Kellogg Pact, has found his inspiration in the same order of ideas that governed apostles of the balance of power. Political methods change, but the objectives remain the same. In essence, the traditional aims of France, the aims which she has today, center about the quest of security. And what is that but the maintenance of peace?

To sum up. If in the past France has sometimes given herself over to the spirit of conquest, either she was led to do so in the enthusiasm of victory after attacks had been launched against her, or because she felt that she was carrying the torch of liberty to the peoples of other nations. Even then, in the hours of their greatest triumphs, our statesmen (knowing how quickly the French spirit can change) thought like Talleyrand that the surest foundation of peace lay in the reëstablishment of the balance of power. This view we still hold.

Of course the situation is not precisely the same today as formerly. At Geneva discussions are carried on in public, and for that reason a preoccupation with the principle of the balance of power seems out of date. But it would be a mistake to take this view. There are groups, cabals and oppositions inside the League of Nations, and though political action may take new forms, at heart it is the same. National aspirations are the expression of national interests, and these, as I have said, persist through the ages because human nature does not change. They condition the relations of peoples, and according to circumstances bring them together or set them one against the other. So it was with France and England; they had long been enemies, but they united at last in the face of a common danger. It is true that by the Briand-Kellogg Pact most of the nations have solemnly renounced war, but in 1914 how little the most solemn engagements were worth when the German Chancellor, Bethmann-Hollweg, declared that necessity knows no law! We therefore are under compulsion to neglect nothing which can guarantee us against the danger of war.

When I have said that security has always been the cardinal aim of France, that term must be understood in its fullest sense. There is a France outside our own frontiers. Just as England cannot permit her communications with India to be menaced in Egypt, and just as the United States considers that one of her elementary interests is to safeguard the Panama Canal, just so France must guard her communications with her possessions in North Africa and preserve her freedom of action in the Mediterranean. Here we touch the problem of the relations of states at its most delicate point. For it is when states come into direct contact that practical accommodations become imperative.

Security! The term signifies more indeed than the maintenance of the homeland of a people, or even of their territories beyond the seas. It also means the maintenance of the world's respect for them, the maintenance of their economic interests, everything, in a word, which goes to make up the grandeur, the life itself, of the nation. But all peoples have not the same ideal; each follows what it considers to be its national interests in accordance with its own traditions. If the nations are to live in peace, those who direct the foreign affairs of each state must try diligently and long to understand and respect the aspirations of others. For by a statesman's comprehension of the forces which direct the destiny of nations one measures the breadth and depth of his genius.

CHAPTER II

GERMANY

By Richard von Kühlmann

OF all the great evils inflicted upon Germany by the disastrous end of the World War, the break in the historical tradition of her development was perhaps the most damaging. The final collapse at the end of the gigantic struggle, the disappearance of the monarchy and of the governing classes, shook the state to its foundations. A considerable time was bound to elapse before out of the chaos following defeat, disappointment, poverty and suffering anything like comparative stability could be again evolved. Unwise measures imposed by the victorious Powers at the time of the Versailles Treaty, and afterwards, made matters worse. After a long time of uncertainty and party struggles, President Hindenburg appointed Adolf Hitler as Chancellor of the Reich. The overwhelming approval which his policy received at the subsequent Reichstag election seems to warrant the hope for a national government with a promise of continuity and stability.

It must seem venturesome to attempt to point out the permanent bases of foreign policy for a country which in its present form as a united nation looks back on an existence of less than seventy years. The task is the more difficult since forty years after the unification of the Reich decisive changes took place in the map of Europe. However, if we investigate the matter more closely we find that, after all, geographical position and historical developments are so largely determining factors of foreign policy that, regardless of changes in the form of the national Government, the foreign policy of a country has a natural tendency to return again and again to the same general and fundamental alignment.

France, whose problems of foreign policy have been so brilliantly discussed by M. Jules Cambon, one of the oldest and most experienced of European diplomatists, may be cited as a pertinent example of what has been said. Since the last quarter of the eighteenth century, the forms and principles of government as well as the ruling classes have undergone more frequent changes in France than anywhere else in Europe. Nevertheless, it was not a mere phrase but the very truth when M. Thiers, during the National Assembly at Bordeaux in 1871, was able to affirm that the admirable continuity of French history throughout manifold changes in régime has been the chief source of strength of this mighty, vehement and restless nation.

Italy, to quote another example, found some permanent elements of her foreign policy laid in her cradle, as it were, by her position between the Mediterranean and the Adriatic. It is on this account that her foreign policy concerning several highly important groups of questions (notably her relation to the ruling sea Power, England) has been forced into permanent channels.

But, as already pointed out by M. Cambon, perhaps the most striking example is that of the Russian Soviet Republic. Probably no newly instituted form of government has ever before gone to such lengths in overthrowing, changing and turning upside down the established order of things as the Soviet Republic. The process is carried so far that, in many cases, even considerations of state policy have to give way when not in complete accord with the party doctrine. But notwithstanding all this, a bird's-eye view of the foreign policy of the Soviets shows astonishing similarities to the foreign policy of the Tsarist Empire. In Asia, above all, the leading idea of indirectly furthering purely Russian political aims by supporting local nationalistic movements has been followed out by the communistic republic to the same extent as under the Tsars. The external aspects of things may change, the intensity of application may vary, but the guiding principles remain the same.

The difficulty of pointing out the permanent bases of German foreign policy is due to several reasons. The German Reich of today is a very young political entity. There is still a generation living which witnessed its foundation. Sixty years is not a great age for a state, nor a long enough period for forming solid traditions.

Considering that, up to its expulsion in 1866, Austria practically had the hegemony in the German Confederation, logic would seem to suggest that one might first search Austria's foreign policy in its larger aspects for influences or principles of a permanent nature which could be regarded as equally enduring and authoritative for the guidance of the German Empire. But the most superficial examination suffices to show that the Vienna cabinet had to contend with too many anxieties and aspirations in other directions, in Italy and along the Adriatic, in the Balkans, in Poland, to render the history of its policy very illuminating in regard to the present aims of German foreign policy. Austria's attempts to secure German support for aims essentially foreign to German interests—attempts such as were made, for example, during the Crimean War with great vigor and considerable skill—played an essential part in estranging Germany from Austria and in preparing the way for the final parting.

Nor is the policy pursued by rising Prussia, around which the new German Empire was built up, as instructive with regard to permanent guiding principles as might be thought at first. Prussia owed her ascendancy in the first place—it would be foolish to deny it—to a line of eminent princes, among whom Frederick the Great was the most gifted and the most brilliant. Her position between the Great European Powers—England, Russia, Holland, France and the Hapsburg realm —forced her, if she was to survive and develop, into perpetually changing combinations, treaties and alliances, too manifold and diverse to be reduced to a formula applicable to the new Germany.

We are therefore compelled to seek for light as to the permanent bases of Germany's foreign policy in her geographical position and in her diplomatic history since the foundation of the Reich.

The only natural frontiers of the Germany we know today are to be found to the south and the north. In the south the rampart of the Alps forms a barrier which, since the days of the Romans, has permitted only insignificant changes. To the north, Germany borders upon two seas, the North Sea and the Baltic. The North Sea forms part of the Atlantic main; but in many respects, and especially from the military view, it is hardly more than an inland lake, for the naval power of Great Britain blocks the way to the high seas. The Baltic, linked as it is with the outer world only by the narrow Danish straits, is an inland sea. While eminently suitable for local trade, it has never been able to play a significant part in a struggle for world power.

Apart from these practically immovable boundaries in the north and south, Germany is unprotected by natural frontiers. In the west, it adjoins France, a country completely unified ever since the time of Louis XI and welded together into a massive block by its culture, its customs, its language and its history. As early as the seventeenth and eighteenth centuries, this most gifted, most restless, most ambitious and most warlike nation of the Continent directed the powerful momentum resulting from its national consolidation against the only open continental frontiers which it possessed—against upper Italy, where the eastward course of the River Po provided a military highway and battlefields; against upper Germany, where the same remark held good as regards the valleys of the Danube and the Main, which also run from west to east; and against the Lower Rhine, where increased elbow-room seemed to beckon. No wonder, then, that poor discordant Germany, torn a thousand ways, suffered heavy losses of area, nor that even today there are prudent and provident Frenchmen who regard it as possible and desirable that the Rhine should form the frontier against Germany.

Germany's eastern frontier has suffered radical changes in consequence of the treaties terminating the war. Prior to the war, this frontier from Upper Silesia southwards adjoined the Austro-Hungarian Monarchy, that is to say, a friendly and allied country, while northwards, and up to the Baltic, it touched Russia. Today, the southerly half of this eastern frontier borders on the newly created republic of Czechoslovakia, a state still animated by violent anti-German feelings on account of its old resentment against Austrian rule: associated, moreover, with

France in the closest diplomatic and military alliance.

Russia's relations with Prussia and Germany before the World War were friendly rather than hostile, and her support in serious crises—during the Napoleonic wars, as well as in the wars of 1866 and 1870 which created the German Empire—was always of inestimable value to the Hohenzollern dynasty. Today, this powerful friend, whose sympathies could perhaps not always be counted on, but whose usefulness had been demonstrated by the events of history, has been replaced by the Polish Republic, another new commonwealth.

So much for the frontiers of Germany. Let us now consider her internal arteries. The rivers of Germany, on account of their size and their importance for commerce and traffic, are of the greatest significance not only as waterways, but also because of their valleys.

For sentimental reasons, the first place among German rivers is accorded to the mighty Rhine, rich in legendary lore; to this region more than to any other the Germans are attached with heart and soul. Throughout its whole course, with the exception only of Alsace-Lorraine and of the estuaries, which are held by the friendly Dutch, the Rhine is a German river, washing German shores and fostering German economic life. But great as has been its emotional and cultural significance since the days of the Romans, the Rhine valley has never given rise to the formation of a large political unit. Small political entities, such as free cities and ecclesiastical principalities, glorious enough in their cultural development, have always prevented the Rhine valley from attaining any decisive political significance as a whole.

The same is true of the Main, the most important tributary of the Rhine on the right bank. Its source is in German soil, and all its long winding course is entirely through German territory. The Main forms a right-angle with the Rhine, and the junction is one of the most vital spots in Germany.

Whereas the mouth of the Rhine since olden times has been in the hands of the Dutch, a Low-Saxon tribe and thus related to the Germans in language and customs, though independent for many centuries, the mouth of the Elbe is entirely under German control. Not far distant arose the illustrious Hanseatic town Hamburg, whose name, together with that of Bremen, is symbolical of Germany's important overseas interests.

Flowing for the most part in the same direction as the Rhine and the Elbe, *i.e.*, largely from south to north, are the Vistula and the Oder, two other German rivers which should be mentioned here. Emptying into the Baltic, which must be regarded altogether as an inland sea, as was already pointed out, they have never been able to aspire to the importance of the rivers flowing into the German ocean.

Among all the great rivers of Germany, the Danube next to the Rhine wears the richest garland of legend and history. The great heroic epic, the Nibelungen, was sung on its shores. Thus does a song of tragic import mark the beginning of German literature. Taking its rise not so very far from the Rhine, the Danube flows in a parallel but opposite direction to that of the Main and almost in a straight line from west to east. But only its upper reaches wash German soil. Since it is navigable as far upstream as Ulm, the Danube has always formed one of the most important routes for trade and for the migration of peoples. Near Passau it receives the waters of the river Inn, which has its source far away in the south. Its green and limpid waters carry southern manners, architecture and implements into the valley of the Danube, thus adding to the Danube's own rich culture—sprung from the meeting of east with west—new and diversified elements of yet another origin.

In this way, Germany's rivers point to her various spheres of interest: the Rhine, the Weser and the Elbe to the ocean and to the wide world beyond the seas; the Oder and the Vistula to Scandinavia and Russia; the Danube to the Near East. These many outlooks make it all the more necessary for the German people to practice the strictest concentration and self-restraint, if the great diversity of their interests is not to lead to a futile splitting up of energies.

In the interior of Germany are mountains, which, while not so very high, are sufficiently difficult of passage to divide the north from the south and to direct the course of development in these two parts along very different lines. Only in the north was there a plain extensive enough to foster the development of a self-contained political unit. Here Prussia arose, and it was Prussia which was destined to become the nucleus of the German Empire.

Prussia was carried to great heights of power and prestige by Frederick the Great, but was temporarily eclipsed through the defeat inflicted by Napoleon. She gained her supremacy in Germany through Austria's secession from the Confederation in 1866 following a war of exemplary brevity. With the support of the other German states she then forced France to assent to the foundation of the new German Reich.

German history since the end of the Middle Ages has for the most part been tragic. Until 1870 cultural and religious disunion combined with the fact that the country was divided into a bewildering number of minute political entities to produce frequent and frightful catastrophes. By far the worst of these was the Thirty Years' War, which left Germany depopulated, impoverished and brutalized. Many generations were needed to extricate the country from its misery.

During the whole eighteenth century, and the first decades of the nineteenth, Germany furnished the military highroad, the foraging ground and the battlefield for the grandiose contest between the House of Hapsburg and France—the France of kings, of revolutionary generals, and of Napoleon. These pages of Germany's history are also written in blood and tears. The overthrow of Napoleon terminated the terrible wars of the French Revolution and of the First Empire, which are to be regarded essentially as the continuation of the gigantic struggle between England and France for naval supremacy, as well as of the old rivalry between France and the Hapsburgs. It was left to the Congress of Vienna to effect the reorganization of Europe and of the rest of the world; and notwithstanding all the criticism to which its work has been subjected, one cannot withhold respect for what was achieved by those diplomats of the old school. For to all essential purposes, the conditions established by the Congress of Vienna lasted a century, right down to the World War.

A brief glance at one of those historical charts on which the war periods are tinted red shows what a peaceful century the nineteenth was: how small the number of wars, as compared with previous centuries, and how short their duration. This largely explains why mankind was able to make such astounding progress during that period, and why the peoples of Europe were able to enjoy such a visible increase in civilization, prosperity and comfort.

The last quarter of the nineteenth century witnessed simultaneously the unification of Germany and the unification of Italy. These developments marked the beginning of radical changes in the European equilibrium, changes which ultimately caused the monstrous coalition war of the years 1914 to 1918.

Germany's complete collapse after her heroic struggle against practically the whole world ended in the Peace of Versailles. There probably are few thoughtful statesmen today who would deny that, among all the peace treaties terminating the great wars of coalition fought during the past three centuries, the Treaty of Versailles was the least satisfactory and the least wise. To transform it into something practicable and supportable is the main task of the present generation. For, conspicuous and deplorable as its defects may be, one must not forget for one moment that the Peace of Versailles, together with its supplementary agreements, now constitutes the basis of public law in Europe, and that its disappearance would be bound to result in a murderous war of all against all.

Germany's central position in the heart of Europe is chiefly responsible for the disastrous reverses which have been so frequent in her history. They have balked her progress at every step, nipped every growing bud, doomed every hopeful development to a tragic ending. No one ever recognized this more clearly than did Bismarck himself. He saw that owing to her central position Germany might at any moment be endangered and overwhelmed by powerful coalitions, and the thought cost him many sleepless nights. The *cauchemar des coalitions* with which a Russian diplomat once teased the Prince was anything but an imaginary nightmare. Rather was it his clear realization, based on history and experience, of the fact that a terrible danger continually hung over Germany's head. Viewed in this light, the foreign policy of the great chancellor, which sometimes seemed so complicated, becomes astonishingly clear and lucid.

As long as there has been any French foreign policy at all, France has held to the principle that no unified Power must be allowed to grow up in Central Europe. In accordance with this tradition, she was bound to oppose by force the attempt to create a united and unified Germany. This united Germany was nearer home, more rigidly disciplined, better organized and more dangerous than Austria could ever have become. And the struggle against the Hapsburgs had been long and difficult enough.

The unification of Germany therefore could not have been achieved without the war of 1870. And even after it had been achieved, France—or at least the French statesmen of the old school—could see no other aim for the foreign policy of the French Government than to smash to pieces this unwelcome growth in Central Europe. In other words, German policy, as Bismarck understood it, had always to reckon with French hostility as a given factor. The cardinal aim of German foreign policy after the foundation of the German Empire centered in the endeavor to make Germany as strong as possible by alliances with countries whose fundamental interests did not conflict with her own, and at the same time to make it as difficult as possible for France to conclude such alliances herself. This simple cardinal idea was to be realized in the complicated system of alliances which included the Triple Alliance and the Re-insurance Treaty with Russia side by side. As long as he remained in power, Bismarck succeeded in carrying his system of insurance into effect. It is an open question whether he would have been able to continue it after relations with Russia had changed in so many respects.

His successors completely misunderstood the cardinal idea of his policy. None of them was alive to the fact —and even today there are probably not many who have an inkling of it—that the splendid façade of Bismarck's German Empire was the façade of an unfinished building, and that the most dangerous crisis had not yet been passed so long as there remained unsolved the question as to what was finally to become of the diverse peoples loosely joined together in the Austro-Hungarian Monarchy, including several millions of Germans. Not until this problem had been solved could Bismarck's Germany be regarded as having definitely passed out of the danger zone; not until then could it be said to be consolidated and established.

People allowed themselves to be dazzled by the brilliant exterior, by the enormous progress made in all spheres of national life, by the bustle of the day. Fundamental problems were lost sight of in the excitement over ephemeral questions. There is no other explanation for the fact that Germany did not renew the Re-insurance Treaty, that St. Petersburg was goaded beyond endurance by the Baghdad railway as well as by the ever-increasing German activities in Turkey, and that the emphasis placed on the construction of the German battle squadrons forced England more and more into an attitude in which she could be counted upon as a powerful ally of a continental coalition against Germany. In this way the ground was prepared for the erection of the most awe-inspiring coalition which the world has ever seen. In this way the great war of history came to be fought, ending in the catastrophe of 1918-19.

It was perhaps a more terrible lesson than any other nation ever received, and its purport is that Germany, poor and bled white as she now is, has to find her way back to the principles regarded by Bismarck as absolutely indispensable even when she was strong and flourishing. In other words, she has to return to a policy of extreme caution, ruled perpetually by the one guiding principle: to prevent the formation of powerful new coalitions against herself.

Many things have been radically changed by the Peace of Versailles and by the foundation of the German Republic. In diagnosing the future development, one cannot afford to omit a glance at these changes. First of all, let us look at those in Germany herself.

Even under so gifted and frequently self-willed a ruler as William II, the personal direction of foreign policy by the monarch was largely fiction. Leadership in this field in the Third Reich is in the hands of the

Chancellor, the Minister of Foreign Affairs, and to a large extent in the hands of the permanent chief official of the Foreign Office and his expert councilors. The conduct of foreign policy requires an immense amount of knowledge concerning factual and personal matters and a long personal experience. Thus it comes about that persons able to meet these requirements will again and again exert a decisive influence on the course of foreign policy, whether they occupy a prominent position or not. One need only think of the part which Holstein was able to play for a whole generation; nor are parallel cases wanting in other great countries.

A great deal of passion has been expended in declaiming in the press and in other places against secret diplomacy. It is held responsible for many calamities. But, however that may be, it will always remain a fact that the trained diplomatist will already have pulled the levers and set the switches this way and that long before the public is in a position to understand a given situation or to appraise its consequences. In a railway station the trains stand peacefully side by side a few yards apart; yet one of them runs to Paris and another to Moscow. It all depends on the setting of the switches.

There is a widespread and common belief that monarchs and their ministers are inclined to play with thoughts of war, and often even provoke war arbitrarily, whereas a democracy or a democratic régime offers a better guarantee for the maintenance of peace.

It is not sure whether history justifies this conception. Any sound and healthy democracy is bound to be nationalistic to a certain degree, and perhaps it is more sensitive and irascible where questions of honor are concerned than an individual, who always is aware that, in the terrible gamble of war, he risks his crown, his dynasty and perhaps even his head. One can imagine a very great monarch having the courage to yield where aggression is not counseled by vital and material interests but only by considerations of prestige. A public opinion originating in the masses is hardly likely to have the same courage.

Judging by our past experience, the goal of all German efforts in the domain of foreign policy must be security. M. Jules Cambon has given a masterly definition of the security of a state: "Security! The term signifies more indeed than the maintenance of the homeland of a people, or even of their territories beyond the seas. It also means the maintenance of the world's respect for them, the maintenance of their economic interests, everything, in a word, which goes to make up the grandeur, the life itself, of the nation." It will be the permanent endeavor of the German Government, supported by public opinion, to win and maintain this security.

Many people in other countries believe that there are wide sections of the German people who thirst for revenge. This idea is altogether erroneous. During the war it was a most remarkable psychological fact that not only was there no hatred against France, but rather that there existed very generally a feeling of respect which is due a brave adversary. This feeling continued undiminished until, after the war, it was reversed by measures such as the invasion of the Ruhr and blunders in the occupied territory.

For a long time the reparation payments of the Versailles Treaty caused considerable irritation. The question of war debts having practically been shelved by the Lausanne agreement, the question of disarmament became the main topic of diplomatic discussion. The French attempt to maintain Germany forever in a state of complete inferiority, even as regards defensive armaments, has prevented the growth of more friendly feelings. Nevertheless, I am sure I am right when I say that the idea of a war of revenge against France does not enter the mind of the average German. On the contrary, in view of the close business relationship which exists today in many spheres of activity, in view also of the very lively cultural exchange and of the attitude adopted by some far-seeing French statesmen, it does not seem at all improbable that notwithstanding temporary resentment and bad feeling France and Germany will find the way to a full and sincere understanding. Such an event would give both states a maximum of security; indeed, it would place the peace of Europe on a new and permanent foundation.

Germany's relations with the Hapsburg Monarchy

were always of a special nature. Prince Eugene of Savoy, the friend of the Duke of Marlborough, not only one of the greatest captains but also one of the greatest statesmen of his period, laid down as a guiding principle of his policy: "There should be a perpetual alliance between the houses of Austria and Brandenburg. This alliance must contain the stipulation that neither of the contracting parties has the right ever to dissolve it." From the Napoleonic Wars up to 1866, Austria-Hungary must be regarded as forming part of Germany. In 1866, it is true, a short and sharp passage of arms was unavoidable in order to crowd Austria-Hungary out of Germany and to achieve the final unification under Prussian leadership. But so unparalleled and so intimate was the feeling of fellowship that, on the very battlefield of Königgrätz, Bismarck pondered on the possibilities of future cooperation. And indeed, not long afterwards, the German Empire and the Austro-Hungarian Monarchy were united by an alliance of the very closest sort.

In a Europe in which all the important states were set up on a purely national basis, so heterogeneous a conglomeration as the Hapsburg Empire, with different parts which constantly betrayed centrifugal tendencies, could not exist permanently. The final dismemberment of this venerable but decrepit empire will probably be described by future historians as the true purport of the World War. Of all the sins of the Versailles Treaty, Austria is the most deadly.

The peace treaties have left of that empire a torso which bears the name Austria. Each neighbor took whatever the treaties permitted or expediency counseled. What still remained forms the Austria of today. Whether a viable state can be made of this fragment is one of the outstanding problems which has worried European diplomatists ever since peace was concluded. The future alone can give an answer to this question. On racial and historical grounds Germany is so closely related to Austria that she will always feel for the people of Austria a special warmth and cordiality. Even in times of acute tension between the two governments the ties of blood relating the peoples will endure. The relations between Germany and Austria will be as close as times and circumstances permit. To achieve a solution of the Austrian question, satisfactory to all concerned, will remain one of the permanent aims of German foreign policy.

To the east, Germany borders on Czechoslovakia, one of the "Succession States" which arose out of the ruins of the former Hapsburg Empire. Czechoslovakia was and still seems to be ruled by a violent aversion to everything German. The historical explanation of this feeling is probably to be sought in the hatred for Austria where the German element was preponderant. Germany and Czechoslovakia are not separated by any acute territorial questions. Nor are there any serious conflicts of economic interest. Indeed, valuable as the French backing may be to the Czech Government, it is not difficult to imagine a development of European affairs which would make it highly advantageous to Czechoslovakia to cultivate good relations with Germany—something by no means unattainable from the standpoint of sound practical politics.

There were and still are serious difficulties with Germany's more northerly neighbor, Poland, whose territory was principally carved out of the Russian Empire, with the addition of former Austrian and German provinces. Not only is there the memory of former friction to overcome, not only is the pronounced nationalism and passionate temperament of this gifted nation to be reckoned with; above all stands the fact that the Peace of Versailles created most unfortunate frontiers between Germany and Poland. It must be stated quite frankly that these frontiers injure the vital interests of Germany so profoundly that the revision of them will remain a standing demand of German foreign policy, no matter who happens to be responsible for its conduct. There is no one in Germany, however, who thinks of war or of the employment of force in this connection. The conviction was bound to gain ground in Poland herself that in the long run it would be suicide to live in open enmity with both her great neighbors. Far-seeing Poles understood that France, placed before a choice between Russia and Poland, would decide for her old pre-war ally, Russia. The courageous initiative for better Germano-Polish relations came, as far as we know, from Chancellor

Hitler himself. A *modus vivendi* between the two states has been established and public opinion has gratefully welcomed on both sides of the frontier the lessening of tension. The symptoms of more friendly feelings in both countries are numerous. This may be considered a good omen for the future. It is certainly possible to work out readjustments which would take account of German national necessities without prejudicing any vital interests of Poland. Her political and military alliance with France is still in existence, but relations between the two nations seem for the time being to have cooled considerably. Well-informed French observers say they have no delusions about the future attitude of Poland.

The disarmament question still lies across the whole European situation, and events in Austria in 1934 have filled with anxiety the hearts of all those who want to see peace maintained.

As far as Soviet Russia is concerned, the student of foreign policy is beset with peculiar difficulties. For notwithstanding all denials, intelligent and experienced observers are quite correct in maintaining that the whole state machinery is completely dominated by a single political party, and that this party regulates even the conduct of foreign policy from the standpoint of party politics. Every sober student must conclude that world revolution is the cardinal and definite goal towards which the Soviets are working today with every means at their disposal. That is why it is extremely difficult for other countries to establish satisfactory diplomatic relations with Soviet Russia, or to maintain them once they have been established. Russia has been skilful and successful in improving her diplomatic position. The greatest victory since the establishment of the Soviets has been the recognition by the United States of America, opening up new possibilities for dealing with the Far Eastern question. Another great achievement is the practical renewal of the pre-war alliance with France, which has forced the Balkan States to abandon diplomatic opposition to Moscow.

Good relations with Russia are one of the oldest traditions of Prussian and German policy. Frederick the Great recognized their paramount importance. From the Napoleonic Wars until after 1866 and 1870, the successes achieved by Prussia and Germany would have been hardly conceivable without Russian backing. On his deathbed the Emperor William I enjoined his successors to cultivate friendly relations with Russia. If it had not been for internal changes in Russia, and undeniably also for grave blunders in German foreign policy—one need only think of the non-renewal of the Re-insurance Treaty and of over-zealous German political activity in Turkey and Western Asia—the old relationship could never have been destroyed so completely as to allow the idea of a Russo-French war against Germany and Austria to become prevalent in St. Petersburg.

Germany's plans in Turkey and Western Asia have

been definitely destroyed by the Great War. Apart from the difficulties arising out of the peculiar political structure of the Soviet Republic, as referred to above, there is no conflict anywhere at present between German and Russian interests. Economically the two countries can be of great service to each other. Moreover, since (as has already been pointed out) the cultivation of good relations with Russia may be described as perhaps the oldest and strongest tradition of German politics, any political régime in Germany, whatever its name or character, will be strongly inclined to carry it along. Probably it would be a mistake to believe that the renewal of the Russian alliance with France must necessarily mean strained relations between Moscow and Berlin. There is a natural antagonism between Hitlerism and Communism. On the other hand, Soviet diplomats are much too shrewd not to know that the value of their alliance with France will only be enhanced if there exists the possible alternative of a more pro-German attitude.

Germany's most important neighbor in the south is Italy, although the territories of the two are nowhere directly contiguous. Italy's attitude during the war caused bitter disappointment in Germany. But as she had joined the Triple Alliance only after receiving England's blessing, and as the configuration of the Italian coasts made it impossible for her openly to antagonize England, one really had to be very shortsighted and optimistic to believe that Italy would fulfil her obligations as an ally in a coalition war in which England was among the opponents of the Triple Alliance.

At the present time, if we omit the difficulties connected with conditions in what was called South Tyrol, there is only one conflict of interest between Germany and Italy, *i.e.*, that arising out of the Austrian question. Italy seems to have made it a principle of her foreign policy that Germany must not gain paramount influence in Austria, that eventually she would oppose such a development by force. Against this must be put in the other side of the balance a number of considerations which ought to make closer relations desirable to both. Under the astute and energetic leadership of a dominating personality, Italy has undoubtedly succeeded in improving her standing among the nations. Her relations with Hungary and Austria are intimate and confidential enough for us to presume that the influence of those two states, combined with that of the Catholic Church, will be sufficient to keep her from overplaying her hand in the South Tyrol. It is probably correct to say, too, that there are powerful elements in German political life which would favor an approach to Fascist Italy and to her friends just mentioned.

Germany's relations with England, like those of Prussia before, had been friendly up to the Great War. The dynasties of the two countries were closely related. Aside from temporary friction caused by the expansion of Germany's commerce and shipping, and in part also by German colonial aspirations, England observed a benevolent attitude toward the foundation of the German Empire and toward the system of alliances by which Bismarck intended to safeguard it.

In the end, it was principally the accelerated construction of the German battle fleet which induced England to side with Germany's adversaries. This point of friction has been completely removed as a result of the war. The new Germany has no intention of building—nor would it be able to build—a navy that could be regarded as a menace to England.

During the years just before the war, the British Government had clearly shown by its attitude in the negotiations then under way that it was clever and far-sighted enough to allow Germany to take her share in the tasks of European civilization, especially in Africa. This field offers possibilities today no less than in former times for an understanding between the British and German Governments. Bismarck had the good sense to make it possible for France, after her serious defeat in the war of 1870–1871, to enter upon extensive colonial activities. Obviously it would be equally sensible to open the same sort of a safety-valve for the vigorous and (in the younger generation) somewhat explosive energies of post-war Germany.

Harmonious and friendly relations have existed between Germany and the United States ever since the time of Frederick the Great. Even the war was able to injure them only temporarily. America has cooperated more vigorously than any other country in the economic reconstruction of Germany, and the intensive exchange in the cultural field has now been taken up again. Here again there are no vital antagonisms of any kind and, on natural as well as on historical grounds, further developments ought to be along friendly lines.

The history of Franco-German relations during the last few centuries is a history of continuous great wars. We have already seen how France, having attained unity at an early time, was able to deprive Germany, split up as she was into small discordant states, of important territories; how Germany was involved, if only as a minor partner, in the great struggles between England and France and between France and Austria; and how in the end she had to fight for her own unification in a brief but bitter war with France, whose traditional policy it had been since Richelieu to prevent at all costs the formation of a strong state in Central Europe.

France fought her war of revenge for 1870–1871 during the years 1914–1918, and carried her success further by an adroit policy of alliances. But the purpose of this war, as influential French statesmen saw it in those years—*"l'écrasement définitif et complet de l'Allemagne"*—has not been achieved. Out of the collapse Germany has saved the better part of Bismarck's work, *i.e.*, her unity as a state; and the further course of events, notwithstanding repeated checks and interruptions, makes it possible to predict with confidence that Germany will succeed in healing her grievous wounds and finally will emerge from the catastrophe as one of the Great European Powers.

As far as a German observer can judge, there is no unanimity today in leading French circles. Some French statesmen believe, with poor enough logic, that the *sécurité* which they regard as their highest political aim can be achieved only by confining and oppressing Germany. They are oblivious of the fact that such a policy is bound to conjure up the very dangers which they seek to avoid. French oppression has more than anything else contributed to Chancellor Hitler's overwhelming success in Germany. On the other hand, there is a group of far-seeing and judicious men who believe that the safest and wisest course would be to grant the former adversary conditions which make it possible for him to live, so that this inheritance of war, carried on through the centuries with changing fortunes, may be brought to an end once and for all.

This result is necessary if the two countries, and with them all the states of Europe, are not to bleed helplessly to death. Public opinion in France has been nervous over various events in the field of German domestic politics. It would be idle to prophesy about future developments. But one thing is certain. Transcending all fluctuations of variable elements, one of the strongest and most persistent endeavors of German policy will be to achieve relations with France which will make it possible for both peoples to devote themselves to their national tasks in a dignified manner and in perfect security. Chancellor Hitler again and again has stretched out his hand to the Western neighbor. If this endeavor could become a permanent factor in the foreign policies of both these great nations, so close to each other in many respects, the forecast for the future of our continent might be drawn in hopeful terms, and peace with honor might at last become Europe's heritage.

CHAPTER III

GREAT BRITAIN
By Sir Austen Chamberlain

NOTHING in foreign comment on British policy surprises an Englishman more than the frequent attribution to British statesmen of all parties and in all times of an almost machiavellian subtlety in the design and an unalterable persistence in the execution of their plans. Such a picture of ourselves seems to us to lack even the resemblance of a caricature to the original, and to attribute to the conduct of our foreign relations the one characteristic which, whether for good or evil, it most conspicuously lacks. Yet the charge is constantly made—sometimes as a reproach, sometimes with admiration and almost with envy—and as certainly believed. What is the explanation and wherein lies the truth?

Both are perhaps to be found in a characteristic of British psychology. The German is by nature a systematizer. He excels in organization. He likes to see where he is going, to foresee as far as may be the accidents of the route and to be assured of good accommodation at the end of his journey. "According to plan." How often did not the phrase recur during the war in German bulletins? "The plan" was at once their security and their danger—often their most efficient instrument but sometimes their master. The Englishman on the other hand finds such systematic planning irksome and uncongenial. He submits himself to it with reluctance even when circumstances impose it on him and, even while submitting, he distrusts the process in which he is engaged, doubts his power to pierce the mists of the future, and secretly relies on his capacity to meet emergencies as they arise. In difficult times there is no more common ending to a political discussion between Englishmen than the phrase: "Well, I suppose we shall muddle through somehow." It could never occur to a German or a Frenchman to seek consolation in such a reflection.

The difference is indeed as marked between the mental processes of Englishmen and Frenchmen, and here the contrast has been drawn with delightful humor by an observer of much experience and complete impartiality. "Two peoples," writes Professor Madariaga, "closely allied by ties of race and language, whose long intimacy of peace and war might have been expected to develop an accurate mutual knowledge, will offer us an unrivalled illustration of the psychological obstacles which beset all international work. . . . France and England are often in Geneva at loggerheads. Not that their interests cannot be made to agree. As national interests go, their differences are more often than not bridgeable in themselves, given a little time and good will. Thus it is not altogether impossible to bring the French and the British delegates to see eye to eye. Only that their eyes are so different. . . . Time and again I have seen the French nonplussed at the illogical and empirical vagueness of the English, and the English shocked and irritated at the unseemly yet unreal clarity of the French." "The whole difficulty," he continues, "comes from the particular region in which the center of gravity of their respective psychologies is situated, which in the Frenchman is above, and in the Englishman below, the neck. The Frenchman thinks with his head, and with nothing but his head; the Englishman thinks—or rather, as he himself says, 'feels somehow' with everything but his head, and, provided he does not allow his head to meddle with it, he is generally right." [1]

When I first met with this passage I happened to be Secretary of State for Foreign Affairs. It struck me as so acute an analysis of the characteristic mental processes of two nations which have so much difficulty and yet so great a need to understand one another that I permitted myself to read it to the Permanent Under-Secretary of State, later British Ambassador in Washington. He did not resent it or deny the soft impeachment. On the contrary he exclaimed, "Isn't that good? I see myself. I constantly come into your room

[1] Salvador de Madariaga: "Disarmament." New York: Coward-McCann, 1929.

GREAT BRITAIN

and say: I have a sort of a feeling that this would do or that wouldn't." And we laughed as we looked together into the mirror which Professor Madariaga had held up to our English nature.

"The Frenchman," says Professor Madariaga, "trusting thought, is apt to distrust life and therefore he endeavors to imprison future life in present thought; while the Englishman, who trusts life and mistrusts thought, refuses to foresee and is content to cross the bridge when he comes to it—even at the risk of having to ford the river on finding that there is no bridge at all."

It results from these different psychologies that it is, or should be, much easier for a German or Frenchman to state his reasons for a course of action than for an Englishman. In the case of a German it is the result of "a plan" and easily develops into a system; in the case of a Frenchman it is the consequence of a logical process of thought, leading irresistibly to equally logical conclusions. But the Englishman follows neither process. He distrusts logic at all times and most of all in the government of men, for instinct and experience alike teach him that men are not governed by logic, that it is unwise to treat political issues as exercises in logic, and that wisdom more often lies in refraining from pressing sound arguments to their logical conclusion and in accepting a workable though illogical compromise. After all, logic lost us the Thirteen Colonies.

Recognizing in ourselves this distaste for systematic thought and this inherent distrust of long-prepared solutions, we are at a loss to understand criticisms which impute to us schemes we have never entertained and a sublety of thought of which we feel ourselves incapable. We are not ashamed of being called empirical; we admit—we may even boast—that we are guided less by logic than by instinct and we are prepared to confess that when we "feel somehow" that a certain course is wise or right, we are apt to take it without more ado. If you ask the average Englishman, therefore, what are the permanent bases of British foreign policy, he will probably reply that there is nothing permanent about it, and, if pressed further, say: "Oh, I suppose Peace. We are 'a nation of shopkeepers,' you know." If you want more, he will have to think.

Yet there must be some foundation for the very opposite view taken by foreign observers and, perhaps, such underlying unity as exists in British foreign policy is more perceived by a foreigner than by a native, just as family likenesses are quickly recognized by strangers, whereas members of the family circle see only the individual differences.

If, then, we are to find some influences permanently at work in moulding British foreign policy, we must surely seek them in causes which are equally permanent. The influence of geography on history is a commonplace of modern thought and the geographical situation of Great Britain has been in fact the dominant factor in determining her development whether consciously planned or, as has happened far more often, instinctively pursued.

Three geographical facts have been decisive for the course of British history and explain, just as they dictate, the main principles of British policy and the preoccupations of British statesmen. First, Great Britain is an island, but, secondly, this island is separated only by a narrow streak of water from the Continent of Europe. Thirdly, this island has become the center of a wide-flung empire whose arterial roads are on the oceans and through the narrow seas.

Great Britain is an island state. She has no land frontiers. Her pretensions to become a continental Power, to expand as her rivals were expanding, by continental conquest or inheritance, were finally settled by the Hundred Years War. Since then she has looked to the sea as at once her defense and her opportunity. Her land forces have been kept at a minimum. They have never been sufficient to wage a continental war except in alliance with some great military Power; but, thrown into the scales on one side or the other in a struggle between the continental giants, their weight and the bull-dog tenacity of the race when once engaged in a fight have more than once been decisive of the issue. At sea, on the other hand, she has—until these latter days when she has admitted American parity—jealously guarded her naval superiority, for to deny the passage of the narrow seas to her enemy was her only defense, to keep them and the oceans open to her own ships was a necessity of her daily existence and a condition of her imperial power.

But though Great Britain is an island, detached from the Continent and prone to regard herself as unaffected by those cares which occupy the first place in the minds of the inhabitants of continental countries, the waters which divide her from western Europe are so narrow that she can never for long remain indifferent to what happens on the opposite shores of the Channel or the North Sea. Steam brought the coasts nearer and rendered the movement of ships independent of the winds which played so large a part in the days of Nelson and Cornwallis. The development of aeronautics has further impaired our insular security and has given fresh force to the secular principle of British policy that the independence of the Low Countries is a British interest, that their frontiers are in fact our frontiers, their independence the condition of our independence, their safety inseparable from our own. It was to secure the independence of the Low Countries that we fought Spain in the sixteenth century, that we fought Napoleon in the nineteenth and that we fought Germany in the twentieth. Here, at any rate, we find a permanent basis of British policy, recognized and reaffirmed by the guarantee we have given in the Treaty of Locarno to the frontiers of Germany and her neighbors on the west.

"The treaties of Locarno," wrote Mr. H. A. L. Fisher, Warden of New College and formerly Minister of Education in the government of Mr. Lloyd George, "correspond exactly with this conviction. Let it be clearly understood that it is not against Germany that the Treaties of Locarno, which form the existing basis of British policy in Europe, are directed. The British guarantee, a factor of the first importance in the political orientation of the new Europe, is a support only for the Power which loyally observes the limits prescribed by the Treaties of Peace. It is neither France, nor Germany, nor Belgium which is the eventual enemy indicated by the Treaties of Locarno. The enemy is the aggressor whoever he may be. It is therefore not in the interest of any one Power or of a group of Powers nor of the balance of power in Europe that these treaties were made. The great object was the peace of the west. If you seek the ultimate cause of this great diplomatic act, you will find it in the necessity of composing the quarrel between France and Germany, of tranquillizing public opinion and of giving to France and Belgium such a feeling of security as will facilitate the reduction of armaments and the restoration of individual and commercial prosperity." [2]

[2] H. A. L. Fisher: "La Politique Etrangère de la Grande Bretagne." Conférence faite à la Fondation Universitaire de Bruxelles, 1929.

I add that to bring Germany into the League of Nations and so secure to her her rightful place in the counsels of Europe was a not less essential feature of Locarno in the eyes of the British Government. More than one hundred years before, at the close of the Napoleonic wars, Castlereagh had renewed the Quadruple Alliance directed against any recrudescence of danger from France and had then secured the association of France in the counsels of the four Powers which formed it. "To give France her Concert, but to keep our security" were the words by which he described the aim of British policy. Substitute Germany for France and the definition held good for his successors a century later. There is, after all, some continuity in British foreign policy.

There have been times in her history when England has sought to free herself from all interest in or dependence on the affairs of the Continent, but they have never lasted long nor has the result of such isolation, whether "glorious" or not, been encouraging. Nature has placed our island too close to the shores of Europe for us to remain unaffected by the storms which burst there, whilst the development of communications and the course of scientific invention have increased our vulnerability. There are many who would be glad to see England as free from European entanglements as the United States, though, as the Great War shows, even America may be involved by a general European conflagration. But for us the peril is closer, the danger more imminent, and we best insure against it not by abstention until war has actually broken out but by throwing our weight beforehand into the scale of peace. It is at least arguable that, if the German Government had known for certain in 1914 that Great Britain would join France and Belgium in resistance to any aggression, the Great War would have been averted. It may be added that a deliberate and purposeful abstention from all part and interest in continental affairs is the one course of policy which might provoke a European combination against us by driving France into the arms of Germany and causing both to heal their quarrels at our expense.

It is true that the Great War had its immediate origin in the murder of the Archduke in Bosnia and it is of course possible that a cause equally remote might again involve the Western Powers in conflict. This is an argument which has often been invoked by continental nations, and occasionally by a section of British opinion represented by Lord Cecil, as a reason why we should extend our guarantee to other and more distant frontiers—as, for instance, by assuming the additional responsibilities of the Geneva Protocol of 1924. Exponents of this view argue that the wider our guarantee the less the probability that we shall ever be called upon to implement it, which is something like saying that if only you ask enough ladies to marry you, you need never marry at all. But this view has never commended itself to the British people and it has found still less favor with the Dominions.

Only in the case where her interests are immediately at stake and where her own safety must be directly affected by the result of any change has Great Britain ever consented to bind herself beforehand to specific engagements on the Continent of Europe. Her attitude was defined in a passage of the statement on the Protocol of 1924 which was read by the British Foreign Minister to the Council of the League of Nations in March of the following year:

> Since the general provisions of the covenant cannot be stiffened with advantage, and since the "extreme cases" with which the League may have to deal will probably affect certain nations or groups of nations more nearly than others, His Majesty's Government conclude that the best way of dealing with the situation is, with the coöperation of the League, to supplement the covenant by making special arrangements to meet special needs. That these arrangements should be purely defensive in character, that they should be framed in the spirit of the covenant, working in close harmony with the League and under its guidance, is manifest. And, in the opinion of His Majesty's Government, these objects can best be attained by knitting together the nations most immediately concerned, and whose differences might lead to a renewal of strife, by means of treaties framed with the sole object of maintaining, as between themselves, an unbroken peace. Within its limits no quicker remedy for our present ills can easily be found nor any surer safeguard against future calamities.

The Treaties of Locarno were the definite embodiment of this policy in the public law of Europe. For the rest, the influence of Great Britain is used everywhere, and particularly at and through the League of Nations, on the side of peace; but if war should nevertheless break out, she has no special obligations apart from those which are common to all the states members of the League of Nations except her ancient Treaty with Portugal and the Convention of the Straits. The Portuguese Treaty embodies a guarantee of the Portuguese Colonial possessions but it is held that Great Britain is sole judge of the occasion and the extent of any assistance she might feel called upon to give. The Convention of the Straits is an outcome of the Great War and is of interest as redefining the British position in regard to the approaches to Constantinople and the Black Sea. But both documents must now be read in connection with the Covenant of the League and it is to the League that Great Britain would today address herself in the first instance if trouble arose in either sphere. Great Britain, indeed, now takes the League as the foundation of her foreign policy and finds in the development of the League's influence the best guarantee of peace and, consequently, the best security for British interests. Her rôle at Geneva, as interpreted by successive governments, has been, whilst remaining faithful to old friendships, to seek a reconciliation with former enemies, to act as a link between the Great Powers and to help where she can to bring them together—as France and Germany at Locarno, and, later, Italy and France in the naval conversations at Rome and Paris. Above all it has been the endeavor of British statesmen to prevent Europe from falling back into two hostile camps. Her own relations with most of the Powers are and have for some time been excellent. British advice is often sought, and I think it is fair to claim that its impartiality is recognized and that it accordingly receives a gratifying measure of consideration.

An exception to this general statement for some time was Russia. The Labor Government renewed the diplomatic relations which were broken off by their predecessors after a long series of provocations patiently borne and warnings constantly ignored. But though ambassadors were exchanged, relations remained uneasy. The two Governments were not agreed upon the meaning of the document which they had signed, and Mr. Henderson was driven to protest more than once against breaches of the agreement. Great Britain makes no pretension to dictate the form of government which other nations shall adopt, but she expects that nations with which she is in formal relations shall abstain from interference in her domestic affairs, shall respect her institutions, and not excite to enmity against her either at home or abroad. For some years it could not be said whether the Soviet Government would decide to conform to those established rules of international comity without which formal diplomatic relations are a sham. However, the simultaneous menace to Russian interests from Japanese ambitions in the

East and from Hitlerite Germany in the West produced a sensible change in the Russian attitude towards Europe. Whilst Germany and Japan withdrew from Geneva, Russia showed an increasing wish to cooperate with the League of Nations, and in the autumn of 1934 was formally accepted as a member. Not less significant of her changed attitude was her proposal for an "Eastern Locarno," which was subsequently given its reciprocal form in conversations between Sir John Simon and Foreign Minister Barthou which took place in London.

The amended proposal, which at once received the hearty approval of Signor Mussolini, offered by far the most important contribution to the peace of Europe which had been made since the original Treaty of Locarno. We were indeed warned by Sir John Simon not to call it an "Eastern Locarno" but an "Eastern Pact of Mutual Guarantee" and no one will be disposed to quarrel about a name, but the purpose of the new proposal was the same as that of the earlier treaty, namely to assure the peace of a defined and limited area by "knitting together the nations most immediately concerned, and whose differences might lead to a renewal of strife, by means of treaties framed with the sole object of maintaining, as between themselves, an unbroken peace."[3] It was made clear that neither the United Kingdom nor Italy would be a signatory of the proposed Eastern Pact or in any way

[3] See the British forecast of Locarno already quoted.

68 THE FOREIGN POLICY OF THE POWERS

extend their commitments under the original Locarno, but the British Government, with the approval of all parties in the House of Commons, made public their view by the mouth of the Foreign Secretary, "that an Eastern Pact of Mutual Guarantee, based on the strictest principles of reciprocity and conceived with the genuine purpose of strengthening the foundations of peace in Europe—I will go further and say strengthening the foundations of peace in the world—by creating a further basis for reciprocal guarantees, is well deserving the support of the British Government and of the British people." [4]

Thus, in spite of the fact that this proposal was nipped in the bud by the refusal of Germany and the reluctance of Poland to participate, the Locarno spirit lives and works in unexpected moments and unlikely places, and once again we have seen a serious effort to underpin the Covenant by local agreements instead of attempting to create a new superstructure which its foundations might be unable to bear. This development was the more interesting because in the two years before it occurred there were moments when a casual observer unversed in our history might have thought that this country was reverting to the idea of isolation. A fierce attack was made in a limited but strident section of the press against all European entanglements and we were bidden to free ourselves from the obligations of Locarno and

[4] Sir John Simon in the House of Commons, July 13, 1934.

even from the Covenant of the League of Nations. For a time it was difficult to determine the exact measure of sympathy given by public opinion to this campaign. It has since become clear that it was wholly unrepresentative. Leaders of all parties have repudiated it and have reaffirmed the loyalty of Britain to her engagements. The Treaty of Locarno emerges from the discussion as the visible embodiment of the principle which has for centuries determined British policy in Europe and must continue to inform it.

"Of course," said Sir John Simon in the speech from which I have already quoted, "the integrity of Belgium is no less vital to the interests and safety of this country today than in times past. It is a geographical fact which nothing can change. Indeed changed conditions, especially in relation to the air, have not altered that historic fact at all; they have only served to emphasize it. That is the point of view of our own national security." Again, on July 30, 1934, Mr. Stanley Baldwin spoke as follows: "Let us never forget this: since the day of the air, the old frontiers are gone. When you think of the defense of England, you no longer think of the chalk cliffs of Dover; you think of the Rhine. *That is where our frontier lies.*" The permanence of this basis of national policy could not be more authoritatively declared.

I have dealt so far with the consequences of Great Britain's insular position on the very fringe of the Continent of Europe. Even here her policy is always influenced and sometimes conditioned by the existence of the Empire across the seas. Outside Europe the maintenance of her imperial communications and the interests of the Dominions, colonies and dependencies become dominant. But for India and the Dominions of Australia and New Zealand, there would have been no British occupation of Egypt, no reconquest of the Sudan for civilization, and the great work accomplished by Lord Cromer and his assistants would have remained unattempted. The fact that Egypt commands in the Suez Canal the main artery of communication between England on the one hand and India and Australasia on the other is what took us to Egypt and keeps us there. We cannot afford to see Egypt and the Canal dominated by another country any more than the United States could tolerate the domination of the Panama Canal by a foreign Power. We cannot therefore allow abuses or disorders to arise in Egypt which would justify or excuse foreign intervention; but, subject to this over-riding necessity, it is the policy of Great Britain to leave the management of Egyptian affairs as far as possible to the Egyptians themselves, and to confine our interference to the defense of our vital interests and the discharge of our obligations to other nations to whom we have formally declared that we should regard any interference by them in the internal affairs of Egypt as "an unfriendly act" and "any aggression against its territory as an act to be repelled with all the means at our command."

In the Sudan the conditions are somewhat different. We were responsible for its reconquest from the devastating tyranny of the Mahdi and his successors, and we pledged our word to its people that the old misrule of the pashas should not be restored. Here, therefore, we have a direct and immediate responsibility to the people themselves for the form and character of their government, and we claim and exercise the power necessary to fulfil our pledge. The Condominium has been maintained. The British and Egyptian flags are hoisted together over the Government buildings at Khartum, but since the murder of Sir Lee Stack, Egyptian troops and officials have been withdrawn and all effective control has been in British hands.

Passing to the Near and Middle East, we find that here also the permanent basis of British policy is fixed by the existence of the Indian Empire. No British Government desires to extend its liabilities in the Red Sea, the Persian Gulf or on the shores of the Indian Ocean, and, indeed, in Iraq we reduced them as rapidly as the circumstances of the case and our mandatory obligations to the League of Nations would admit; but the safety of our communications is vital to us. With no aggressive intentions ourselves, we shall be content if no other Power cherishes aggressive designs. Our interest lies only in the maintenance of peace and of the *status quo*. Stable governments, able to defend their independence and to preserve their territory from attack, best serve British interests alike in Iraq, Persia and Afghanistan. The experiment of dividing Persia into Russian and British spheres of interest, though made in the interests of peace and in the hope of preserving the integrity of Persia, was not a success. The war put an end to it and it is never likely to be revived.

Passing now to the Far East, it may be said that our relations with Japan from the moment of the rebirth of that island empire were of the most friendly and cordial character. The alliance concluded in 1905 was finally terminated in 1921 after its terms had been modified on an earlier occasion, both the modification and the final termination being made out of deference to American sentiment; but the relations of the two countries, though no longer those of allies, remained cordial until cooled somewhat by the action of Japan in Manchuria, her withdrawal from the League of Nations, and the sometimes obscure but none the less disquieting expositions of Japanese policy in regard to China and the Far East generally. The British Government's attitude is now one of waiting watchfulness. The purpose of British policy remains unchanged but the method of its expression may be altered to meet the altered character of Japanese aims. It is too soon to forecast what the turn of events may bring forth; but if I were to hazard a prediction, it would be that the course of British policy will be largely determined by that of the United States and by the extent of the understanding which it may be found possible to establish between our two nations in a sphere where their interests are identical. Their coöperation might indeed be the determining factor in preserving the independence of China and the peace of the Pacific Ocean.

The interests of Great Britain in China are entirely commercial. There, more than anywhere else, our policy is the policy of "a nation of shopkeepers." At no time have we cherished any territorial ambitions, at no time have we desired conquest or annexations. Throughout the troubled years which preceded and have succeeded the Boxer rebellion the object of British policy has been to safeguard the integrity of China and to preserve the open door for traders of all nations; and here, as elsewhere, British interests would best be served by the establishment of a strong national government able both to preserve internal order and to protect Chinese territory from external aggression.

His Majesty's Government were a party to the decisions of the Washington Conference of 1921. They were not responsible for and they deeply regretted the long delay which occurred before the Tariff Conference assembled in Peking, and the failure of that Conference to reach agreement. In particular they viewed with grave concern the proposals then made by certain Powers that foreign control over the customs revenue of China should be tightened and extended instead of being relaxed as was contemplated at Washington. Meanwhile, China had become a prey to civil war, the authority of the Peking Government had almost disappeared, and a powerful Nationalist Government was in process of establishment in the south. In these circumstances the British Government of the day defined their policy in a statement published in December 1926, in the course of which they said:

> During all these civil wars it has been the consistent policy of His Majesty's Government to abstain from any interference between the warring factions or rival Governments. Despite the disorders which civil war engenders and the grievous losses inflicted on the vast commercial interests, both Chinese and foreign, His Majesty's Government have declined to associate themselves with any particular faction or to interfere in any way in the civil commotions. His Majesty's Government believe that the Powers have adopted a similar attitude and that this is and will continue to be the only right attitude to maintain.
>
> The situation which exists in China today is thus entirely different from that which faced the Powers at the time they framed the Washington treaties. In the present state of confusion, though some progress has been made by means of local negotiation and agreements with regional Governments, it has not been possible for the Powers to proceed with the larger programme of treaty revision which was foreshadowed at Washington or to arrive at a settlement of any of the outstanding questions relating to the position of foreigners in China. The political disintegration in China has, however, been accompanied by the growth of a powerful Nationalist movement, which aimed at gaining for China an equal place among the nations, and any failure to meet this movement with sympathy and understanding would not respond to the real intentions of the Powers towards China.

His Majesty's Government, after carefully reviewing the position, desire to submit their considered opinion as to the course which the Washington Treaty Powers should now adopt. His Majesty's Government propose that these Governments shall issue a statement setting forth the essential facts of the situation; declaring their readiness to negotiate on treaty revision and all other outstanding questions as soon as the Chinese themselves have constituted a Government with authority to negotiate; and stating their intention pending the establishment of such a Government to pursue a constructive policy in harmony with the spirit of the Washington Conference but developed and adapted to meet the altered circumstances of the present time.

It is on these lines, uninterrupted by the change of government in England, that British policy has since proceeded. Realizing that the old treaties were out of date and desiring to put our relations with China on a footing better suited to present conditions, we have been prepared to relinquish the special rights secured by the older treaties just in proportion as the Chinese Government is able to replace the security which they afforded by such a system of law, order and administration as will guarantee to our nationals the rights which peaceful traders are accorded in any civilized state. Considerable progress has already been made upon these lines, but the salvation of China can be worked out only by the Chinese themselves, and the rate and extent of progress must be determined by the ability of the Chinese Government to preserve internal security, to protect life and property and to afford foreigners the ordinary guarantees given by a just system of law and its impartial administration.

I have left to the last the consideration of British relations with America, certainly not because they are less important in the eyes of Englishmen than our relations with Europe or the East, but because to treat them fully would require more space than is at my disposal on this occasion, whilst the sole aim and purpose of British governments, from whatever party they are drawn, can be stated in a single sentence without ambiguity or qualification.

It is an axiom of British policy that we should always seek to preserve the most friendly relations with America. Sentiment and interest combine to impose this attitude upon us. War between us is, we hope, unthinkable; it would be a crime not only against our own peoples but against civilization. I can say with confidence, after a Cabinet experience of more than a quarter of a century, that such a possibility has never entered into Great Britain's consideration of her requirements for defense and has never influenced the strength of the forces maintained by her, whether on land or sea. The three-thousand-mile frontier which marks the boundary between the United States and Canada remains unfortified—at once the symbol and the pledge of enduring peace between the British Empire and the United States.

But merely to preserve peace would be a wholly inadequate and negative expression of British policy.

We desire much more than the maintenance of peace. We wish by all means in our power to remove all causes of friction, to wipe out the memory of old quarrels and to place and keep our relations on a footing of cordial friendship and good understanding. It has not always been easy. American comment on, and even intrusion in, English affairs has not always been friendly or even fair. American diplomacy has sometimes been rough and its expression unnecessarily harsh and wounding to a proud though happily not very sensitive nation.[5] No doubt we too have sometimes blundered, failing to take sufficient account of American susceptibilities or to make our own purpose clear or, again, misunderstanding the American point of view. Such errors of conduct or differences of opinion are perhaps inevitable from time to time, but they need not and should not impair our friendship if they are treated on both sides with common sense and mutual forbearance.

It can safely be said that no government will ever command or retain the support of the British people which is thought for a moment needlessly to jeopardize the good relations of the two peoples. It is our earnest prayer that, in whatever differences the future bring forth, we may meet with a like spirit across the Atlantic Ocean.

[5] *Cf.* President Cleveland's Venezuela Message.

CHAPTER IV

ITALY

By Dino Grandi

IF I had been writing this ten years ago I should, no doubt, have sought to show with what lack of understanding Italian problems had been examined and settled at the Peace Conference; and I should have tried to explain the reasons for the deep sense of dissatisfaction with which the Italian people received the results. Today it does not seem necessary to do this. During these ten years the problem of ensuring peace, tranquillity and work, so as to enable a people with limited resources to meet the ever growing demands of life, has gradually come to be universally recognized. The situation created by those who made the peace terms in Paris is such that a detailed review is superfluous. Public opinion all over the world is beginning to ask how statesmen could have parcelled out immense colonial territories without any regard for the only one of the Allies for whom the pressure of population was creating a vital and urgent problem. How could statesmen, when distributing colonial mandates, have seen fit to entrust these to Great Britain, France, Japan, Belgium, South Africa, New Zealand

and Australia—and none to Italy? Why, at the risk of deeply offending the Italian people, did they choose to create so many artificial difficulties and obstacles to Italy's national aspirations? Why, in short, should Italy, who had been a loyal member of the victorious alliance in the war, have deliberately been thwarted and made discontented?

No doubt errors were committed by the Italian representatives in Paris. But this does not alter the fact that the men who represented England, France and the United States were fundamentally lacking in any understanding of Italian needs. They failed to realize that Italy was a young and active country, entering on a new phase of demographic and economic development, and that she was animated by new spiritual values which were to take shape in a much more vigorous conception of the future of the nation and the rôle of the state. Their failure seems all the stranger when we remember that they possessed the key to the new Italian political situation. Italy was not driven into the war by force of circumstances. Her intervention was her own voluntary act. Before committing the country to such an enterprise, the Government very properly tried to safeguard Italy's rights to compensation at the end of the war. But it was a wave of popular enthusiasm which swept the politicians before it and in 1915 decided upon intervention.

It should not have been difficult to see that this movement, of which Mussolini was the leader, was the outcome of a reserve of youthful energies, capable of giving a fresh and vigorous impetus to national life. The statesmen in Paris, however, were blind to the ideals of the new generation of Italians. They also failed to take a practical view of the Italian question. It was not in the interest of Europe and European stability to debar Italy from the outlet requisite to the growing needs of her population; nor was it a move in defense of the interests of European civilization to offend and humiliate the new spirit of energy animating the Italian people. It was that people, in the sequel, which was destined to make the most vigorous contribution of any single nation to the common defense of European stability and of European civilization.

The greatest lack of understanding of the realities of the Italian situation was displayed by the statesmen of France, and this was the primary cause of the uncertainty and instability prevailing in Franco-Italian relations during the post-war years. The relations of the two countries have been so genuinely improving in recent times that, I trust, I am safe in putting forward these historical considerations without risk of giving offense. There is one page in M. Poincaré's memoirs which it is difficult to read without asking oneself whether political insensibility is not sometimes accompanied by a considerable amount of moral insensibility. I refer to an extract from his 1915 diary, written at the moment when Italy was entering the war as France's ally. After having enumerated the territorial concessions granted to Italy by the Treaty of London, M. Poincaré adds: *"Rien ne prouve, d'ailleurs, qu'au moment de la paix toutes ces attributions puissent être maintenues."* An obscure phrase, perhaps, but one which can be better understood if we read what Ray Stannard Baker wrote in his book "Woodrow Wilson and the World Settlement." In it he records that, a few days after the armistice, the Quai d'Orsay approached Colonel House and proposed "to scrap all the secret Treaties for the sake of curbing Italy." This meant annulling the Treaty of London, which stipulated the compensations due to Italy at the end of the war.

Is it surprising that Italy left the Conference with the feeling that she had been injured in her rights and interests, convinced that she had been deceived and defrauded, and determined to correct these errors and right these wrongs? I persist in calling them "errors" because I have always felt that, from their own point of view, French statesmen—Clemenceau and his followers—whose object it was to create a condition of stability so as to protect the Treaty of Versailles, ought at least to have been wise enough to wish to associate a great country such as Italy with the cause of conservation. It was evident that Italy, being a country in a phase of dynamic development, would otherwise be inevitably drawn towards a revisionist policy.

I do not wish this statement of mine to be misunderstood. Mussolini's foreign policy, in the matter of the revision of the Versailles Treaty as in other questions, rests on a much wider conception than the mere correction, in Italy's interest, of certain of the diplomatic results of the Paris Conference. But the fact that the Italian people has of recent years been peculiarly interested in the question of the revision of treaties is assuredly due in part to its own painful experience at the Peace Conference—an experience which, notwithstanding the radical change that has taken place in Italy's international position during the last few years, is not yet forgotten. The Italian people has always considered that the peace settlement, both as a liquidation of the World War and as a foundation of the new institutions which were to guarantee the future political stability of Europe, was based on an insufficient and erroneous view of the facts. On this point the Duce has expressed himself with his usual clearness and straightforwardness.

Coming into power in October 1922, Mussolini was faced by two exigencies of foreign policy: the need to rouse the European Powers to a sense of Italian realities, to a recognition of the new creative forces inherent in the national rebirth; and the necessity of incorporating the Italian question in the vaster and more general problem of a revision of the principles upon which the peace settlement had been founded.

One episode of Mussolini's foreign policy has often

been misunderstood both in the United States and in England. Indeed, my American and English friends have always advised me not to talk about it. I frequently bring it up, however, because I believe in the eloquence of examples. I refer to the Corfu episode. There is a sentimental aspect to this incident, and apparently that is the only one which struck the imagination of most people: namely, the guns of a great naval Power were trained against a lesser one. This fact is certainly not new in history, nor can it be suggested that Mussolini invented the procedure. Not unnaturally, however, every time it occurs it arouses a reaction of public feeling. But the real importance of the Corfu incident was quite different. The Duce, by the concrete example of the Corfu expedition, called Europe's attention to the respect due the new Italy and to the reawakened energies of the Italian people. That is to say, it called attention to a fact that had been ignored at the Paris Conference.

According to international custom, when a warship wishes to order a vessel suspected of carrying contraband to stop, she shall fire a warning gun. At Corfu the Duce fired his gun, not to intimidate Greece, but to intimate to Europe that it was time to halt for a moment in order to consider Italy's international position, before the tension created in Italy by the wrongs done her at Paris reached the danger point. By so doing, he made the first real contribution to European peace. A few months later the question of Fiume was peacefully settled by a direct understanding with Jugoslavia, the independence of Albania was secured, and the relations between Italy and Greece themselves entered upon a phase of friendship and collaboration. This led to the Italo-Greek Treaty of 1928—an event which I regard as particularly fortunate, and one that displays the intelligence of Greek statesmen, who realized that the Corfu episode was not an Italo-Greek incident, but a stand made by Italy *vis-à-vis* Europe—a somewhat strong one perhaps, but very illuminating. So illuminating was it, in fact, that since then Mussolini has not found it necessary to fire any warning guns against anyone.

He has had other means of recalling Europe to a sense of reality, since Europe—harassed by political instability, divisions and conflicts, revolutions in many of its leading states, and urgent claims beating against the fragile structure of the peace treaties and the League of Nations—has itself come to demand that revision of principles and methods which the Duce for ten years has advocated and fostered.

The Peace Conference bequeathed to Europe two tendencies, both divorced from reality: the apocalyptical ideology of which President Wilson was the primary interpreter; and an out-of-date reactionary spirit whose principal exponent was Clemenceau. One of these tendencies seeks to immobilize Europe in a network of theoretical formulæ, the other to force it into an iron frame based upon past events.

ITALY

While one of these tendencies reflected the past and the other faced towards the future, both, however, had a common significance: the immobilization of history—Clemenceau by the pessimistic notion of French security, Wilson by the optimistic notion of universal peace. Their aims were different, but the starting point, and I might say the initial illusion, were the same. For both sought to suppress the realities of history by denying the free play of the forces of movement and development that make history. The Powers in Paris attempted to force the peace problems of Europe into this duplex structure of unreality. They regarded them not as dynamic problems of the future, the settlement of which demanded careful preparation, but as static questions to be definitely settled by legal and coercive means.

Ever since 1919, Europe has dwelt in this fantastic structure of prophecies and armaments. But while the force of arms has steadily increased, the force of prophecy has dwindled. The League of Nations exists at Geneva; but despite all the trust we may place in it, and all the good will with which we uphold it, it is a fact that the League now stands on the defensive; and all the efforts made for a reduction of armaments have led to no results. Indeed, the Disarmament Conference has meandered into a legal quibble on "parity of rights," from which we are seeking to extricate ourselves by an effort of diplomacy; which all goes to prove the need of reforming the methods with which the League of Nations has worked to the present time.

These methods do not respond to the exigencies of international life. They are derived from those ideological formulæ which attended the League's birth, and from the experiments of the parliamentary system. I do not mean here to discuss parliament as a constitutional institution in Europe or America. It is a fact, however, that the parliamentary system no longer enjoys unanimity of consent nor inspires the universal confidence accorded it in the nineteenth century. But even were this otherwise, the fact of having transplanted the system from national life into the international domain was a performance that calls to mind the act of the Roman general, who having been struck with admiration for a wonderful sundial at Syracuse, had it dismantled and removed to Rome, only to find that the dial did not work in a different latitude. Parliamentary institutions, in fact, are quite out of keeping with a League of Nations. The League does not correspond to any parliament, because every parliament is connected with an executive power, and the League of Nations possesses no executive worthy of the name. If we are to seek an historical comparison, we should turn rather to the Continental Congress— but American historians have dealt too severely with the Continental Congress for me to dare to do so.

Putting aside these theoretical arguments, we are faced at Geneva with the following reality: that the Powers—large and small—carry their difficulties and

ITALY

their conflicts of interests to the League of Nations. These conflicts do not shrink at Geneva: they expand. The Great Powers, in conflict with one another, seek for allies among the lesser Powers and form hostile groups which complicate and aggravate the situation; the small states court the support of the Great Powers, who in order to maintain their diplomatic combinations at once take sides. Thus all the disputes brought to Geneva finish sooner or later, either directly or indirectly, as conflicts between the Great Powers. During my stay in Geneva I never saw a dispute of any importance settled otherwise than by an agreement between the Great Powers. They alone are responsible for the situations that arise. A few states that remain outside of fixed diplomatic combinations, and are therefore able to maintain an independent attitude, have from time to time exercised a conciliatory influence at Geneva. But this only happens in the case of secondary disputes, and, moreover, these lesser Powers, not having at their disposal the forces that might become necessary to back their action, are themselves compelled to have recourse to the Great Powers.

The whole of the Geneva procedure is, in fact, a system of *détours,* all of which lead to one or other of these two issues: agreement or disagreement between Great Britain, Italy, France and Germany—the latter now formally absent, but not yet entirely detached from the League.

Experience and common sense alike prove that political institutions live and function only when they respond to the realities of a situation and are able to adapt themselves thereto. The real situation in Europe is this: the four Great Powers have it in their power to realize a policy of effective collaboration, not only among themselves but also among the lesser states. Every time that the problem has been envisaged in this way—at Locarno in 1925, at Lausanne in 1932, and at Rome during the negotiations for the Four Power Pact—something definite has been achieved. Whenever—as at Geneva during the Disarmament Conference—the Western Powers have departed from this position, the results have been negative, or practically so. It is from this point of view that we should consider the Four Power Pact and the policy defined therein; and it is for this reason that the Duce discerns a close connection between the Four Power Pact and the Locarno Treaty.

"In the Locarno Treaty," he said recently in an historical speech in the Italian Senate, "the position of the four Powers was clearly defined and a basis was established from which in the course of time certain results might ensue. In the years following, European policy has too often departed therefrom.

"It was high time that the four western Powers should return to the principle that had preceded the 1925 agreements and solemnly pledge themselves to collaborate and act in concert and mutual understanding in all questions concerning them; that they should make every endeavor to realize a policy of effective collaboration, not only among themselves, but also with the lesser Powers. It is this pledge that the new Pact solemnly undertakes by Article I, which is the corner stone upon which all the other clauses are based."

Several political observers have thought to discern in the Four Power Pact certain principles tending to reform the League of Nations, and League zealots have criticized it mainly on this ground. It must frankly be admitted that these elements are there. They were already present in the Locarno Treaty, which, after all, created a procedure extraneous to the League, and they are to be found again in the Four Power Pact. Each of these great international treaties sought to establish a system of relations between states which had been paralyzed by the vast and heavy mechanism of the League; and they corrected, or at least they aimed at correcting, those deviations from reality inherent in the universality of the League and in its abstract and ideological character. They sought to remove the League from the world of prophecy to the world of hard facts, from purely theoretical and universal affirmations to the immediate guarantees necessary to satisfy the craving for safety and protection —these are the very words of the Locarno Treaty— that animate the countries who were victims of the war scourge of 1914–1918. Both treaties are the logical expression of the need for common agreement between the four western Powers in order to impart vitality and efficacy to Articles 10, 16 and 19 of the Covenant, and in order to restore the equilibrium that must exist between them if constructive and lasting results are to be obtained.

All this involves a constant effort to adapt the peace treaties to the actual conditions of Europe. For ten years this has been one of the Duce's main preoccupations. For ten years he has constantly sought to convince Europe that the real menace to peace consisted in the excessive rigidity of the endeavor to maintain a system of international obligations, on a basis of psychological and political conditions which were changing from day to day. This is, and has always been, Mussolini's thought. I summarize the matter in what are his own words, so far as my memory serves: "From the moment of the cessation of war—of this war, as of all wars that preceded it—the process of adapting the peace treaties to the changing situation commences. It would be useless and dangerous to conceal the fact that this process exists, and that it has often gone on amid far greater difficulties than would have existed in an atmosphere of greater reciprocal trust and understanding. During the years following 1919, rigid conditions have been enforced and have created an atmosphere of tension; while adaptations and revisions have taken place almost unawares, under the pressure of circumstances that have often threatened Europe's stability, and without producing in the relations of the several states and in the general situation that organic improvement which was aimed at and which ought to have ensued."

In maintaining this attitude, Mussolini has often found himself in open disagreement with those French statesmen who regard peace and security essentially in the same way that Clemenceau did: as a system of juridical engagements and a system of military alliances to maintain rigidly the structure of the peace treaties. An understanding with Italy on these lines was difficult. Nor is it hard to see why. A policy of intensive armaments, completed by a foreign policy of alliances, has been constantly explained by French statesmen as designed to give France military security. I avoid saying that it has been essentially directed against Germany, but certainly it has been based upon the hypothesis of a possible new conflict with Germany. French statesmen, with whom I have on many occasions discussed the question, have constantly said to me: "Our armaments do not concern you; why do you worry about them?"

Herein lies the fallacy. The concentration of a great military force in the hands of a single country —whatsoever the specific purpose for which it has been formed—is in itself a fact of political importance, and therefore it concerns everyone. It may be destined, in the intention of the government concerned, to be employed for a given object and in the hypothesis of a particular conflict; but in everyday life it resolves itself into a form of political pressure which cannot be ignored by any of the peoples or states with interests in the continent of Europe. I have never understood how anyone could possibly imagine that the Duce—who has a big pair of eyes, very wide awake in Italy's interest—could close them to this most obvious fact.

The French themselves, moreover, have done everything in their power to make us consider the question from this standpoint. Why did they in London in 1930 obstinately refuse to recognize the principle, laid down by the Washington Treaty of 1922, of naval parity with Italy? If they had wished to make the political purpose of French armaments quite clear to us, it was only necessary for them to come to a fair naval agreement with us. It is not surprising that the refusal to come to any such agreement—following upon the substantial concessions on our part agreed upon with Mr. Henderson in Rome, and embodied in the so-called Basis of Agreement of March 1, 1931—should have been unfavorably interpreted. More recently, that is to say after the Lausanne negotiations and during the preparation of the Four Power Pact, French statesmen have displayed a better understanding of the Italian point of view. Relations between the two countries have consequently improved. The general function of Italy in the balance of Europe is perhaps better understood now in France.

This function is dictated to Italy by her geographical position and her Mediterranean interests. With her natural frontiers, Italy has no dreams of continental conquests; but she must be safe in the continent to which she is attached and on the seas that surround her. This security can only be guaranteed by the equilibrium of European forces. Italy's freedom is compromised the moment this balance is disturbed. Thus Italy cannot be other than adverse to the formation of military alliances, political blocs, and closed systems, which seem to translate into present reality an old civic law of Manu: "Your neighbor is your enemy, but your neighbor's neighbor is your friend." Nor, indeed, do these systems serve to secure the safety of anybody, since by splitting Europe up into so many armed camps they merely exacerbate relations between countries and widen the zones of conflict.

It is to be hoped that with the Four Power Pact —in which the spirit of neighborly collaboration is unequivocal—Europe may take a new turning, and that we may attain a proper balance. I mean a positive, political and military equilibrium, to be realized first of all between the Great Powers, solely because if it is lacking between the Great Powers it is impossible between the smaller. This applies primarily to the question of disarmament.

It is generally known that the Duce holds that disarmament should be achieved by a fair distribution of armaments, which on the one hand would gradually eliminate the great inequalities, both legal and technical, now existing, and on the other would deter Europe from plunging into an armament race. Nor can there exist juridically two different orders of states, one free to arm and the other bound by treaties to a limitation of armaments. Armaments must be placed on a single juridical basis and be equally distributed.

This has been and remains the basic principle underlying Italian policy on disarmament. In which way this principle can be practically applied is a matter of method. In other words, it is necessary to find what immediate and concrete results it is possible to achieve in the actual political situation of Europe. The Duce, in laying down the terms of Italian policy in this field, was inspired by the following principle: that once equality of rights in favor of Germany has been recognized, this principle must be applied. It is necessary to meet Germany's legitimate demands for defensive rearmament. On the other hand, it is also necessary to consider the position of those Powers like France which possess a superiority of armaments; one cannot ask them to renounce immediately and unconditionally all those advantages which they actually enjoy. To do so would be running after shadows, and it would be a departure from and not an approach to that unity of views among the Great Powers without which Europe will find itself shortly plunged into a new armament race like the one which preceded the World War. The Italian Memorandum of January 1934 must be read with this fundamental consideration in mind. It tends to prevent the race to

ITALY

armaments, and to develop a policy of fair distribution of military strength amongst the Great Powers.

In order that such results should be achieved, it is further necessary that the political atmosphere in Europe should become one of confident coöperation between the Great Powers; it is therefore essential that they should renounce all attempts to modify to their own advantage the political balance which has been established. The tendency to concentrate forces—in any form—is equally dangerous. It interrupts the slow, arduous and painful work of reconstructing the political texture of Europe, and it paves the way to a régime of strife and anarchy among the Great Powers. This is exactly what those who drew the Locarno Treaty and the Four Power Pact endeavored to avoid. Attempts to concentrate power—an attempt by Germany to annex Austria would be an example—are the exact antithesis of the Locarno and Four Power Pact policy. They would represent a setback instead of an advance in the policy of revision and would retard coöperation and pacification in Europe.

I think I can express this feeling with all the more frankness inasmuch as everybody knows what cordial and friendly relations exist between Italy and the German Government and people, and how actively Italy has worked in every field (reparations, armaments, etc.) in favor of Germany's equality of rights. This equality should represent an element of balance and of adjustment in the interest not only of the German people but of the whole of Europe. An independent Austrian state is a most essential element in this equilibrium.

In asking for this, Italy does not ask for a guarantee of equilibrium for herself only, but for Europe as a whole. Austria holds a key position on the continent which can be compared only with that of Belgium. There are three crossroads in Europe: one is Belgium, between England, France and Germany; another is Switzerland, between France, Germany and Italy; the third is Austria, between Germany, Italy and the Slav states of southeastern Europe. It is in the interest of Europe that these crossroads be maintained intact, that they be allowed, as political units, to perform their function—that of separating and conciliating the Great Powers, giving them, thereby, that tranquillity and security which are the only foundations upon which a policy of collaboration and peace can be based.

From the North Sea to the Danubian Basin there exists today an uninterrupted chain of political and diplomatic guarantees: the independence of Belgium; the guarantee of the western frontiers of Germany, as stipulated at Locarno; the independence of Switzerland; and the independence of Austria. The preservation of this chain is an essential condition of European collaboration. It is of common interest to the four Great Powers. Hence the close connection, in the mind of the Duce and in Italian policy, between the Locarno Treaty, the maintenance of Belgian, Swiss

ITALY

and Austrian independence, and the Four Power Pact. This is the only system by which the peaceful coexistence of the Great European Powers can be ensured.

There are two countries within this system which are in a similar position and whose interests coincide: Italy and Great Britain. This fact has become more and more manifest in the course of recent years, but I remember the Duce pointing it out very clearly at Locarno, as far back as 1925. "Italy," he said, "occupies the same place as England as guarantor of the agreement, and therefore of the general peace."

It is by no mere chance that Italy and England are entrusted with the same responsibilities in Europe under the Locarno Treaty, and that they constantly find themselves side by side. We have often had differences of opinion with both France and Germany. But on all important questions, such as debts, reparations, disarmament, and reconstruction of the Danubian States, the policies of Italy and Great Britain have always been substantially in agreement. There are permanent interests binding Italy and England together in Europe. These interests are dictated by the geographical position of the two countries, which makes each an interested but detached element of the European situation; by the necessity felt by both countries alike to maintain a certain balance on the continent; and by their respective positions in the Mediterranean.

These interests were realized by far-seeing English statesmen as far back as the beginning of the eighteenth century. England, already in the Mediterranean, sought then to establish closer relations with the Italian states, and more particularly with the House of Savoy; the latter, in order to defend itself against the territorial ambitions of Louis XIV, whom Spain was no longer able to withstand, had for some decades been turning towards England. It is from this period—not as is usually supposed, from the time of Palmerston and Gladstone—that we can date England's first concern for Italian independence. It is from the early days of the eighteenth century that we can trace the English idea of turning to Italy for those elements of guarantee of the European balance which she so anxiously sought.

The affinity of Italian foreign policy with the foreign policy of England grew steadily throughout the nineteenth century and during the early years of the twentieth. The decisive moment in Italian foreign policy, in the early years of the new kingdom, was when, at the moment of the signing of the Triple Alliance (1882), the Italian Government insisted upon the insertion of an additional clause clearly stating that under no circumstances should the Triple Alliance be considered as directed against England. Nor did this suffice: we further demanded a special protocol whereby the Triple Alliance should be left open for British adhesion, at any rate enabling England to adhere to the articles relating to mutual neutrality. This Bismarck opposed, fearing the treaty might take on an anti-

ITALY

Russian significance. Such are the ironies of history! The important point is that the additional clauses, upon which the British-Italian agreements of 1887 were later to be based, permitted Italy to restrict the importance of her continental engagements, and established the Italo-British understanding which has always been maintained.

This understanding has been renewed of late years by the similarity of our views as to the best way of facing Europe's political exigencies, a common dislike for the rigidity of abstract formulæ, and an innate sense of justice in the two peoples—justice based on an understanding of mankind, which alone makes it possible to settle problems in reality and not merely in form. Justice and legality are not identical. There are treaties, pacts and agreements which must be respected and honestly carried out; but over and above treaties, pacts and agreements there are the claims of good sense and equity which must be satisfied. International problems are not merely matters for legal and coercive settlement; they are essentially problems of social order, and social order is maintained only by an earnest effort to satisfy the needs of the peoples.

We are satisfied that during these last years Italy has made this effort. No problem has left us indifferent or lacking in zeal, still less, hostile. Never has Italy refused to recognize the just rights of others. Ever since the signing of the Treaty of Versailles, France has insisted on her need for security. We did not hesitate to guarantee this security, and took a solemn pledge to this effect by signing the Locarno Treaty. The German nation has claimed and still claims freedom. From the close of the war to the present time it is true to say that Italy has never neglected any occasion, however slight, to help Germany arrange for a term to be put to international control over her domestic concerns, to remove over-burdensome obligations in the political, military and financial domains, and to assist the German people to resume its place on an equal footing in the consortium of free nations.

But Italy also has her own problems to solve, and ones no less formidable than those of safety, liberty, and the resumption of economic relations with neighboring countries. Ours is a vital problem that involves our very existence and future, a future of peace, tranquillity and work for a population of 42 million souls, which will number 50 million in another fifteen years. Can this population live and prosper in a territory half the size of Spain and Germany and lacking raw materials and natural resources to meet its vital needs, pent up, moreover, in a closed sea beyond which its commerce lies, a sea the outlets of which are owned by other nations? Meanwhile all the nations of the world are raising barriers against the development of trade, the movement of capital, and emigration, denationalizing whoever crosses their frontiers to enter,

I do not say their own homes, but even their protectorates and colonies.

During the years that Mussolini has been Head of the Italian Government this problem has grown steadily more acute. At the beginning it hardly existed in the consciousness of Europe, which regarded our foreign policy as permanently bound up with and circumscribed by the Adriatic conflict. Today it forms part of the general situation of European reconstruction, which nobody is any longer able to envisage without taking into account the satisfaction of Italy's vital needs.

Thus the first constructive phase of our foreign policy is closed. Fascism has placed Italy's problem before Europe, not as an isolated one to be considered apart from others, but as one factor of the comprehensive European problem, which demands a single organic settlement. In this, I think, consists the deepest and more real significance of the Duce's foreign policy.

CHAPTER V

JAPAN

By Viscount Kikujiro Ishii

EVER since Japan's entrance into the family of modern nations in the middle of the nineteenth century her diplomacy has striven, and still strives, to attain two objectives—equality and security. The first has been almost, but not entirely, attained; the second has for seven decades been the absorbing problem of the nation and will evidently remain such for long years to come.

First let us consider the problem of equality. By "equality" I do not mean that Japan should fall behind no Power on earth in point of wealth, natural resources and military strength—in short, in every respect. Obviously, equality in this sense is as impossible among nations as among individuals. What Japan has insisted upon, what she still insists upon, is that she shall not be made the object of discrimination and derogatory treatment by any of the nations with which she has relations. The full significance of this phase of our policy cannot be appreciated unless we first understand the circumstances in which we entered into intercourse with foreign nations.

When Japan opened her doors to the West seventy years ago, she (like the rest of Asia) had to acquiesce in there being put upon her a stigma of inferiority in the shape of unequal treaties which deprived her of judicial and tariff autonomy. To read into those treaties any sinister designs on the part of foreign Powers, as some ultra-nationalists are inclined to do, is not fair. The Powers, cognizant of the state of our internal administration at the time, and knowing how different it was from their own, did not think it wise or practicable to place their respective nationals under our jurisdiction; though they might, I believe, have been a little more generous in the matter of tariffs. We, on our part, bowed to the inevitable, trusting that the Powers, as soon as we had put our house in order, would remove the extraterritoriality and the one-sided tariff which they had foisted upon us. And, indeed, the "unequal" treaties of 1858 contained a provision for revision by mutual agreement in 1872. When the time came, Japan naturally endeavored to avail herself of this provision. The famous Iwakura mission, which made a tour of Europe and America from 1871 to 1873, had as one of its objects the revision of the treaties. The letter of credence which it carried spoke of an "intention to reform and improve the treaties, so that Japan might stand on an equality with the most enlightened nations." The mission, as far as this object was concerned, was a failure. None of the Powers approached made an encouraging response.

This initial failure proved a blessing in disguise, for it served to spur the Japanese to greater efforts toward internal rehabilitation. From that time on Japan bent all her energies to the modernization of her laws, her courts, her administrative system, her schools, and even her social conditions, to the end that the Powers, recognizing the progress thus achieved, might see their way clear to relinquish the prerogatives they had long enjoyed at the expense of Japanese sovereignty. In 1882, relying upon the reforms which she had introduced, Japan began to negotiate in earnest for treaty revision. And at last, after eleven years of pourparlers with the Powers, she succeeded in obtaining from Great Britain the treaty of 1894 which abolished extraterritoriality.[1] Soon other European Governments followed suit, and by 1900 Japan had practically regained territorial jurisdiction and judicial autonomy.

And yet she was far from having attained equality with the Powers, for she was still bound by a unilateral tariff. Not until the expiration of another period of twelve years was she to recover tariff autonomy and find herself in a position to negotiate reciprocal treaties with other states on a plane of entire equality. It was in 1911 that new treaties were concluded with the United States and Great Britain, conceding to Japan both judicial and tariff autonomy.

[1] The United States had concluded a similar treaty in 1874. But it had remained a dead letter because it contained a proviso that it should not come into effect until other Powers agreed to the termination of extraterritoriality.

It had taken Japan forty arduous years of self-examination and self-improvement to attain the goal.

But our endeavors for equality were not to end with the conclusion of the treaties of 1911. Prior to that a new situation had arisen seriously affecting Japan's position of equality *vis-à-vis* the Western World, in particular the United States and the British overseas dominions. This situation was a result of Japanese emigration to those countries. The American Government, consequent upon the San Francisco "school incident" of 1906, was desirous of excluding Japanese immigrants of the laboring class. Japan, adhering to the policy of equality, objected to such exclusion by an American statute, but was ready to acquiesce in a plan whereby she would of her own accord forbid the emigration of laborers to the United States. The result was the so-called "Gentlemen's Agreement" entered into by an exchange of confidential notes between Tokyo and Washington in 1908. A similar agreement was also entered into with Canada. The basic principle of these agreements was that Japanese immigration should not be openly excluded by a discriminatory law passed by a foreign country, but that Japan would voluntarily check the exodus of her subjects belonging to the working class. As far as the world in general was concerned, the exclusion of Japanese did not exist, and Japan was still permitted to maintain a position of equality in the matter of emigration. Of course, such an equality was hardly more than a fiction; but Japan preferred it to an open discrimination which would run directly counter to the policy which she had pursued for half a century.

The conclusion of the Gentlemen's Agreement did not end the difficulty with America. In 1913 the State of California, in spite of a signal decline of Japanese immigration under the agreement, and in the face of the strenuous objections of the government at Washington, enacted a law denying "aliens ineligible to citizenship" the right to own land. In 1917 it was reënforced by another law which forbade such aliens from leasing agricultural land. Both laws were plainly discriminatory against the Japanese.

At the Versailles Peace Conference the Japanese delegation endeavored to obtain recognition from the Powers of the principle of "racial equality." Baron Makino, acting on behalf of that delegation, proposed the insertion of the following article in the Covenant of the League of Nations: "The equality of nations being a basic principle of the League of Nations, the High Contracting Parties agree to accord, as soon as possible, to all alien nationals of States members of the League, equal and just treatment in every respect, making no distinction either in law or fact on account of their race or nationality."

When it became apparent that such a clear-cut pronouncement could not be adopted, Baron Makino sought to include in the preamble to the Covenant these simple words, "by the endorsement of the principle of equality of nations and just treatment of their nationals." In presenting the above amendment the Japanese delegate laid stress upon the idea that it was not his country's intention to encroach upon the domestic matters of any nation, but that he wished the proposal to be incorporated as a matter of principle. As had been expected, the United States and Great Britain objected to this proposal. On the other hand, France, Italy, Greece, Czechoslovakia and China supported it. Out of the seventeen delegates present, eleven voted with Japan. But when the Japanese amendment was reported to the Commission entrusted with the task of drafting the Covenant, President Wilson, as chairman of that body, rejected it on the ground that it did not meet the requirements of the rule of unanimity, as Great Britain, one of the governments represented in the Commission, had opposed the proposal. This argument was somewhat sophistical, for the rule of unanimity was not then a *chose jugée*, and was to be discussed in the Commission together with the Japanese proposition. Japan's defeat in the fight for equality at Versailles was another set-back to the policy for which she had so long struggled.

But the severest cut of all was the American Immigration Act of 1924, which contained a provision excluding all Oriental immigration upon racial grounds, for the reason that Orientals were not eligible to American citizenship. Ostensibly aimed at all Asiatics, this provision was, in effect, if not intentionally, directed against a single nation—Japan—for the reason that Chinese immigration had long been checked under the Chinese Exclusion Laws, while the Hindus and other peoples of the South of the Asian continent were excluded by another law. Thus in the Immigration Act of 1924 the United States, by a one-sided act, abrogated the time-honored "Gentlemen's Agreement," the object of which had been to forestall just this kind of statutory discrimination.

It should be clearly understood that our primary concern in this respect is not whether or not a few thousand or a few hundred Japanese immigrants shall be admitted to America, but whether Japan shall be accorded the courteous treatment which is due to her as one of the civilized Powers of the world. To us it is a matter of ideals rather than a question of material interest. Ever since we entered into the family of nations at the instance of Commodore Perry, we have spared no efforts toward internal readjustment and reform, so that the civilized Powers may admit us into their circle upon an equal footing. By 1900 they had signified their appreciation of our achievement by restoring judicial autonomy to us; and in 1911 they restored to us tariff autonomy. Only the statutory exclusion of our emigrants by the American Congress stands in the way of our coveted goal of equality. With the American policy of restricting or excluding immigration we have no quarrel so long as that policy applies to all countries without legal discrimination.

In Japan's opinion the common dictates of international justice, international courtesy, and international good will require that no nation shall single out for discrimination any other nation which has by common consent been recognized as one of the civilized Powers of the world. Full appreciation of our disappointment at the exclusion clause of the American Immigration Act is possible only when it is projected against the background of our unremitting toil of seventy years for the realization of our aspiration for equality.

So much for equality. The next question to be considered—that of security—is closely bound up with our history, our geographical position, and our population problem in its relation to our land area, our food supply, and our supply of the essential materials of industry.

For well-nigh three centuries before the advent of Commodore Perry, Japan had isolated herself from the rest of the world by a most rigid policy, forbidding her nationals from going abroad and keeping foreigners from entering her domain. In that long period of seclusion Japan had fallen far behind the nations of the Occident in the arts of war as well as in those of peace. When we were rudely awakened by the impact of foreign guns we found ourselves utterly helpless to defend our country in the face of the formidable men-of-war which seemed to press forward against us from all directions. Thus at the very beginning of foreign intercourse, apprehensions of the superior military force of the West struck deep into our hearts. Our first step towards security, then, was to equip ourselves with the weapons of the West. The necessity and wisdom of this course, in view of what subsequently transpired, especially in our relations with Russia, is clear.

Japan is an island nation. But her distance from the continent of Asia is so small that she cannot be indifferent to what happens in Korea, Manchuria, China and Siberia, any more than England can keep aloof from developments in the Low Countries across the Channel and along the North Sea. Particularly in Korea and Manchuria, we have consistently followed a policy dictated by the sole motive of establishing our own security. We have looked upon their frontiers as our frontiers, even as England looks upon the frontiers of the Low Countries as her own. And as England's policy has been to uphold the independence of the Low Countries so that they may serve as a buffer, so Japan attempted to maintain an independent Korea free from the aggressions of Tsarist Russia. But Korea was neither Belgium nor the Netherlands; she was effete, impotent, and supine. She had none of the moral stamina essential to an independent nation. These are harsh words, but I give expression only to the common verdict of critical observers, both Oriental and Occidental. Into the long and complicated history of our endeavors to preserve the independence of Korea I cannot enter here; suffice it to say that when we found those endeavors unappreciated, futile, and fruitless, we were forced to the only remaining alternative of establishing a protectorate over Korea. This, to us, was the only practicable means of attaining our own security.

In Manchuria, too, we have been actuated by the same motive—security. When that region was in imminent danger of being annexed by Russia in spite of our repeated protests, we were forced to take up arms in defense of China's open door and territorial integrity, a cause championed also by Mr. John Hay, American Secretary of State. We espoused the American doctrine and fought Russia in defense of it, not only because we believed in it but because we thought that it was in consonance with our own policy of security. We saw all too plainly that Russia considered Manchuria a stepping stone to Korea. It was quite possible that in the eyes of Russia even the Peace Treaty of Portsmouth was in the nature of a truce. To Japan the concessions she obtained from Russia by that treaty constituted a bulwark against any possible recurrence of the Russian advance southward, although they had also an important economic aspect, as we shall presently see. These concessions would have come to a premature termination had Japan not concluded the treaty of 1915 with China, as a result of the so-called "twenty-one demands." The significance of that treaty cannot be understood without a clear knowledge of Japan's precarious position in Manchuria *vis-à-vis* Russia, still the military Colossus of the north.

From the standpoint of our security, the Russian Revolution has not materially changed the situation. We still must look to the north with apprehension and a certain sense of danger. M. Jules Cambon has written: "The policy of the Soviet Government in the Far East may differ in method from that which the Tsarist Government followed; but it does not differ from it in spirit or in objective." Sir Austen Chamberlain and Dr. Richard von Kühlmann, both writing on the same theme, have expressed much the same feeling in different language. I am not prepared to say whether these expressions are entirely correct, but I only state what is common knowledge when I say that the vast region known as Outer Mongolia has, under Soviet tutelage and protection, been closed to all but Russians; that even China is not permitted to preserve contact with that region, over which her suzerainty has been formally recognized by the Soviet Government itself; that hundreds of Chinese students, trained in communist schools in the Soviet Union, are yearly sent back to China to promote the communist movement; and that increasingly large regions in China have become the prey of communist risings.

With the internal political system of the Soviet Union we are not seriously concerned. We are on friendly terms with the Union, and are prepared to deal with it in a conciliatory spirit on all problems affecting our mutual relations. But I should be guilty of insincerity if I were not to confess our misgivings as to the activities of the Third International. Its deliberations and plans are most jealously guarded. No one is permitted to get an inkling of them. But one may say without fear of contradiction that most, perhaps all, of the civilized nations outside Russia look upon the deliberations of the Third International, and the activities apparently emanating from it, as disturbing to the general peace and welfare of the world. There is no means of ascertaining the exact nature of the relations existing between the Soviet Government and the Third International; but it is strange, to say the least, that the former, whose avowed foreign policy is peace and friendship, does not seem to exercise any restraining influence upon the latter, whose headquarters are located in the very shadow of the Kremlin.

Nor can the military aspect of the Soviet situation be ignored. Its importance becomes greater in the light of the Soviet Government's attitude towards the Third International. I am fully aware that the military strength of any country is not aimed against any particular foreign nation. Nor do we lose sight of the fact that the Soviet Union, still passing through the critical stage of a political readjustment of an unprecedented nature, needs a large military force for domestic purposes. But our bitter experiences with Russia in the past have caused us to view with apprehension any powerful army imbued with revolutionary ideas looming large on the other side of the Manchurian border.

Generally speaking, our policy in China has been based upon the belief that the establishment of an *imperium in imperio* upon her soil by any powerful third nation or group of nations is not only derogatory to her integrity but is also incompatible with our own security. In this we have been actuated by the same principle incorporated in the Monroe Doctrine. The wisdom of this policy, especially at a time when China seemed to be harassed by endless internal disorders and constant international difficulties, cannot be questioned. We believed that the break-up of China would bring the formidable Powers of the West to our very portals. We thought, for this reason if for no other, that the preservation of China's integrity was essential to our own safety. It was for this reason that we induced China to agree not to cede any part of the province of Fukien to any foreign Power, that we fought Russia in Manchuria, and that we obliged Germany to withdraw from Shantung. For much the same reason we objected to the construction of foreign-controlled railways in Manchuria, though the objection was also based upon the agreement by which China obligated herself not to construct competitive and parallel lines to the South Manchuria Railway.

The most notable example, perhaps, is our opposition to the American project of a Chinchow-Aigun railway of some 700 miles in length. To attribute this opposition to any anti-American feeling on our part is a gross injustice. We protested against it because foreign railway enterprises in China could not be dissociated from international politics. Certainly they were not purely economic in nature. Every student of railway politics in China knows this. I believe in the innocence and good faith of the American promoters concerned; but I am equally convinced that the Chinese Government which invited them to Manchuria had it in mind to undermine the position which we had secured as a result of the harrowing war with Russia, or to embroil us with the American Government. Suppose that the project had been carried out, suppose that China had disregarded her obligations in connection with it and that the railway itself had, as was more than probable, been seized by war-lords. What would America have done then? I am most reluctant to presume that the American entrepreneurs would have succeeded in persuading their government to send troops to Manchuria to protect their interests. But in the protracted chaos in China who shall say that such an eventuality could never have happened? Diplomacy must adopt a long view and take into consideration all possible contingencies.

In detail and in actual application the Japanese policy opposed to the establishment of foreign *imperia in imperio* in China may have been somewhat different from the operation of the Monroe Doctrine in the western hemisphere, but the basic motives have been the same. The difference in application has arisen largely from the fact that by the time Japan felt herself influential enough to champion the territorial integrity of China, that country had already become so helpless in the face of foreign aggression that Japan, from sheer motives of self-preservation, was constrained to entrench herself in some of the regions from which she had ejected the aggressor. This was notably the case in Manchuria. No one believed that China could defend herself against the all but certain recrudescence of Russian aggression after the Manchurian war of 1904–5.

So far I have approached the question of our security from the strategic standpoint. No less important is the economic view. I shall not invoke statistics and marshal figures to prove how vital Manchuria is to us economically. Much has already been written on that subject. It is enough to say that the increase of our population, the congestion of our country, and our lack of raw materials are such that Manchuria, with its virgin soil and its immense natural resources, has come to be regarded as our vital protection. Given unobstructed access to those resources, we may still hope to solve our embarrassing population problem. We do not necessarily mean to promote mass emigration to Manchuria; rather, we shall foster our industries by utilizing the raw materials which we can obtain there. Just as England solved her population problem by industrializing herself, so does Japan hope to solve her similar problem. Such was the object of the Sino-Japanese treaty of 1915, though it had strategic significance also.

The attainment of this objective, however, presupposes the willingness of whatever government rules Manchuria to respect our treaty rights and our position in the region and to take into consideration our interest in the task of economic development envisaged by the 1915 treaty. All that we desire is that it shall observe treaty obligations and shall coöperate with us for our mutual benefit. I am more than convinced that had China taken this attitude of "live and let live" before it was too late, the deplorable incident of September 1931, with all its consequences, would never have happened. All that we had asked of China was the simple observance of the treaties she had duly made—treaties which were and are essential to our security, both strategic and economic. More we did not ask; less we could not take.

The vital importance of Manchuria being generally appreciated by the people, it is all the more difficult for us to recede from the position we have attained there. In a constitutional country, with parliament and the press representing or responding to the popular will, the government is not in a position of itself to determine a course of action when that course involves the national security; it must consider public opinion. I agree with Dr. von Kühlmann when he questions the soundness of the view that "a democracy or a democratic régime offers a better guarantee for the maintenance of peace." As this German statesman puts it, "any sound and healthy democracy is bound to be nationalistic to a certain degree, and perhaps more sensitive and irascible where questions of honor are concerned than an individual. One can imagine a very great monarch having the courage to yield where aggression is not counseled by vital and material interests but only by considerations of prestige. A public opinion originating in the masses is hardly likely to have the same courage." In Manchuria our question is not merely one of prestige, it is one of life or death. This is the general conviction of the people.

The appearance of Manchukuo as an independent state has not materially altered our policy, except for such temporary measures as have been taken to meet the readjustments consequent upon the change of government. Pursuing our traditional policy of security, we shall coöperate with any government in Manchuria which, in our judgment, best appreciates that policy and will best coöperate with us. This, and only this, is the guiding principle of our conduct in Manchuria. Today, as thirty years ago, Manchuria is the key to our security.

CHAPTER VI

SOVIET RUSSIA
By Karl Radek

I AM fully aware of the difficulties of the task which I undertake in attempting to give an account of the main lines of Soviet foreign policy and the fundamental considerations which govern it. The first difficulty arises from the fact that the foreign policy of the Soviet Government differs as much from the foreign policy of the other Great Powers as the domestic policy of this first socialist state differs from the domestic policy of the states belonging to the capitalist system. Men and women who accept the capitalist point of view find it just as hard to understand the socialist state's foreign policy as its domestic policy. Moreover, this primary difficulty is increased by several propositions generally accepted in the capitalist world, although even there they are of questionable validity. I mean the theory of the priority of foreign over domestic policy and the theory of the continuity of foreign policy. In order to clear the way for an understanding of the foreign policy of the Soviet Union the reader must attempt to grasp our attitude toward these two propositions. We consider them erroneous because they are in contradiction with generally-known historical facts.

Foreign policy is a function of domestic policy. It solves problems which result from the development of a given society, a given state, under definite historical conditions.

The wars of the era when modern capitalism was born, the wars of Cromwell and Louis XIV, were the product of the struggle for the emancipation of the youthful capitalism, which gained strength under the mercantilist system, from the oppression of the domestic market, largely based on a peasant economy which met the requirements of the peasant and of his feudal exploiter. There was a need for colonies as sources of raw materials and as markets for the produce of young industries, and also for the plundering which provided the stimulus for the growth of manufactures, which became in turn the basis for the eventual development of machine industry. Industrial capitalism relegates the struggle for colonies to the background because industrial capitalism itself creates an immense domestic market as well as immense means of accumulation and has in cheap mass production a magnificent weapon for mobilizing raw materials from the colonies.

The wars of the industrial era served either as a means for breaking through the Chinese wall which separates the backward nations from the capitalist world (the Anglo-Chinese war, the Anglo-American threats to Japan), or as a way for achieving national unity, which means creating a large domestic market for infant industries (the unification of Germany, Italy, the United States).

Under monopolistic capitalism the mad struggle for colonies was again accentuated. In the war of 1914–1918 the attempt was made to re-distribute the world's surface in accordance with the strength of the imperialistic powers which took part in the struggle. The difference between the aims and methods of the imperialistic policy of the twentieth century and those of the foreign policy of the mercantilist era is made clear, despite their superficial similarity, by the consequences of that imperialistic policy. Whereas during the period of manufactures England did everything in her power to prevent the development of industry in the colonies, the policy of modern imperialism is a policy of exporting capital, that is, a policy of exporting the means of production. This policy, regardless of the intentions of its originators, leads to a certain degree of industrialization in the colonies—although the survivals of feudalism and the exploitation of the colonial countries hinder the process of industrialization and prevent emancipation. The revolutionary movement in the colonies, centering as it does around the young proletariat, shows how different are the policies of mercantilism and imperialism. The fate of India, the fate of China, furnish the proofs.

Where, in this process, is the priority of foreign policy and where is its continuity? Its aims are seen to be shaped by the economic and political structure of changing forms of society. Therefore they are not permanent but, on the contrary, variable.

The attempt to represent the foreign policy of the Soviet Union as a continuation of Tsarist policy is ridiculous. Bourgeois writers who do so have not grasped even the purely external manifestations of this policy. It used to be an axiom of Tsarist policy that it should strive by every available means to gain possession of the Dardanelles and of an ice-free port on the Pacific. Not only have the Soviets not attempted to seize the Dardanelles, but from the very beginning they have tried to establish the most friendly relations with Turkey; nor has Soviet policy ever had as one of its aims the conquest of Port Arthur or of Dairen. Again, Tsarism, or any other bourgeois régime in Russia, would necessarily resume the struggle for the conquest of Poland and of the Baltic states, as is doubtless clear to any thoughtful bourgeois politician in those countries. The Soviet Union, on the contrary, is most anxious to establish friendly relations with these countries, considering their achievement of independence a positive and progressive historical factor.

It is silly to say that geography plays the part of fate, that it determines the foreign policy of a state. Tsarist policy originated not in geographical conditions, but in the privileges of the Russian nobility and the demands of young Russian capitalism. The questions raised by geography are dealt with by each social formation in its own way; that way is determined by its peculiar economic and political aims.

We are thus led to the first fundamental question: What are the aims which may and must be pursued by a society which is building up socialism and which is based on socialism?

I shall not attempt to give here an historical survey of the foreign policy of the Soviet Union. Suffice it to recall that when the Soviet Government came to power it set out promptly to rescue the country from the conflagration of the World War; and that having achieved this purpose at a heavy price it was forced for about three years to defend its independence against the intervention of the leading imperialistic nations, an intervention due partly to the desire of these to drag the Soviets back into the World War and partly to their desire to destroy the first government of the workers, which the capitalist world looked upon as a gross provocation to the capitalist system. This fact compelled the Soviet Union to give a preliminary solution to the problem of defense which had been forced upon it. But even in this early period Soviet foreign policy displayed clearly its fundamental lines, which are fully in harmony with the foreign policy of the socialist system.

The main object for which Soviet diplomacy is fighting is *peace*. Now this term "peace" is much abused. There is no diplomat whose official pronouncements do not use this term reverently over and over again, even though he is a representative of one of those imperialistic nations which are most active in preparing war. But those who are incapable of understanding the specific place occupied by the struggle for peace in Soviet foreign policy are altogether incapable of understanding that policy in whole or in part. Why is the struggle for peace the central object of Soviet policy? Primarily because the Soviet Union—to use the expression of Lenin—"has everything necessary for the building up of a socialist society."

As early as 1915 and 1916 Lenin, then preparing the struggle for the seizure of political power, maintained that it was possible to build up socialism in Russia. He saw the country's vast size, its immense natural resources, and that it possessed a degree of industrial development which would insure, on the one hand, the leadership of the working class and, on the other, provide the minimum of technical knowledge necessary for starting socialist construction.

In Lenin's lifetime the Soviet state, having victoriously ended the war against intervention, took up the work of reconstruction, re-building the industry that had been destroyed and establishing normal relations with the peasantry. These normal relations assured the proletariat the supply of raw materials and foodstuffs necessary for the expansion of industry, as well as the support of the peasant masses. Lenin's successor at the helm of the Soviet ship of state, Stalin, deciding the course of this ship, set as its object the building up of socialism within the borders of the former Empire of the Tsars. This object seemed utopian, not only to the capitalist world, but also to a group inside the Communist Party which followed Trotsky and rejected the fundamentals of Lenin's policy.

In this inner party struggle the policy of Stalin was victorious; and his victory found its realization in the Five Year Plan. This plan has already been put into practice. Its achievement consists in the creation of an industry on such a large scale as to provide the solution of three problems. In the first place, it allows the Soviet Union to proceed independently with the further development of its industry, that is to say, in case of necessity, without importations from abroad, because under the Five Year Plan the Soviet Union has acquired a powerful heavy industry and machine-building equipment of all sorts.

Thanks to the solution of this first problem, the working class can now—and this is the solution of the second problem—provide the peasantry with a number of machines sufficient to prove to even the most backward groups of peasants the advantage of collectivization. On the basis of collectivization it became possible to liquidate those classes of the peasants which were pushing agriculture in the direction of capitalism. The economic annihilation of the kulaks and the creation of an agriculture which has for its chief driving power the products of large-scale machine industry—tractors, reapers and other agricultural machines—owned by the workers' state, has created a situation which the peasantry can and must develop in the direction of socialism. The peasant today is still in an intermediate stage between the position of a small owner and that of a member of a society carrying on a collective enterprise with the help of means of production owned by the society. But it is already perfectly clear that as a result of the advantages of tractors, electricity and oil, over horses, ploughs and scythes, the well-being of the peasantry will depend in increasing degree on the productive forces of the socialist society and not on labor arising from privately-owned means of production. Within the peasant ranks, too, differentiations in productive and economic standards will be abolished, and the peasantry will gradually be transformed into a uniform socialist mass. The economic lot of the peasants will continue to improve, and year by year they will grow closer to the proletariat. This result is guaranteed not only by the increasing industrialization of the countryside, but also by the fact that industrialization is a means for raising the cultural level of the village to that of the urban proletariat. The solution of this second problem—the collectivization of farming—in conjunction with the solution of the first problem—industrialization—makes possible the accomplishment of the third object of the Five Year Plan, namely the creation of conditions which assure the national defense of the Soviet state.

This capacity for national defense is based on the creation of a heavy industry which provides the country with all the means of defense essential to success in modern war, and on the disappearance of all social classes hostile to the up-building of socialism. These classes have been defeated, even though remnants still survive and even though the psychology of the small owner, inimical to socialism, cannot disappear in all groups of the population at once. But if we ask the question, what is the general trend of development, it is clear that the fulfilment of the Five Year Plan and the development of the program of reconstruction in the Second Five Year Plan have proved that the Soviet Union, having laid down the foundations of socialism, is capable of proceeding to build up the complete structure of socialism, the integral socialist society, that is, a classless society which bases itself on all the discoveries of modern technique and that assures to the masses of the population social and cultural conditions of a type which capitalism cannot possibly achieve.

Does the Soviet Union need war in order to build up socialism? It does not. Certain capitalist circles have stubbornly asserted since the Soviet Union was founded that it would seek a solution of its difficulties in war; these assertions are repudiated by its history. Even at the moment when we were particularly ill-equipped to undertake the building-up of socialism, immediately after we had assumed governmental responsibilities, we readily accepted the heaviest sacrifices in order to give peace to the country. We deeply believed—and this was of great importance—that we had in our hands everything necessary for building up a socialist society. Now we know that the problem of building socialism in the Soviet Union admits of a practical solution and that a considerable part of the problem has been already solved. The peace policy of the Soviet Union therefore rests on the granite foundation of triumphant socialist construction.

The enemies of the Soviet Union attempt to undermine the importance of this fact from two directions. Some of them accuse the Soviet Union of having given up its international aims. These aims, in their opinion, would demand military intervention by the Soviet Union to aid the emancipation of the international proletariat and of the colonial peoples. Others, on the contrary, maintain that, because the Bolshevik Party which controls the Soviet Union is inherently an international party, all the peace declarations of the Soviet Union are purely provisional and hence that having reached a certain economic level which enables it to wage an aggressive war the Soviet Union will repudiate its peace declarations and assume the initiative in a war. The best way of answering both these accusations is to quote the statement made by Stalin in December 1926:

This is what Lenin actually said: "From ten to twenty years of sound relations with the peasantry, and victory on the world scale is assured (even despite delays in the growing proletarian revolutions); otherwise from twenty to forty years of sufferings under the White terror." ("Leninski Sbornik," Vol. IV, p. 374.)

Does this proposition of Lenin give ground for the conclusion that "we are utterly incapable of building up socialism in twenty or thirty years?" No, it does not. From this proposition we can derive the following conclusions: (a) provided we have established sound relations with the peasantry, victory is assured to us (that is, the victory of socialism) within ten or twenty years; (b) this victory will be a victory not only within the U. S. S. R., but a victory on the world scale; (c) if we fail to gain victory within this period this will mean that we have been defeated, and that the régime of the dictatorship of the proletariat has given place to the régime of the White terror, which may last twenty to forty years.

And what is meant by "victory on the world scale?" Does it mean that such a victory is equivalent to the victory of socialism in a single country? No, it does not. Lenin in his writings carefully distinguished the victory of socialism in a single country from victory "on the world scale." What Lenin really means when he speaks of "victory on the world scale" is that *the success of socialism in our country, the victory of consolidating socialism in our country, has such an immense international significance that it (the victory) cannot be limited to our country alone but is bound to call forth a powerful movement toward socialism in all capitalist countries*, and even if it does not coincide with the victory of the proletarian revolution in other countries, it must in any event lead to a strong proletarian movement of other nations toward the victory of world revolution. Such is the revolutionary outlook according to Lenin, if we think in terms of the outlook for the victory of the revolution, which after all is the question in which we in the Party are interested.[1]

Such are the fundamentals of the Soviet peace policy.

The socialist society which is being built up in the Soviet Union has foundations already well established and its completion assured. It does not need war. This fact found expression in the Soviet proposal for a general disarmament by all the capitalistic Powers, first advanced at the Genoa Conference while Lenin was still alive. It has subsequently been the axis of the peace policy of the Soviet Union at the Disarmament Conference. This Conference required years of preparation and already has been engaged on its sterile deliberations for two years. Its fate magnificently proves the truth of Lenin's thesis that "under capitalism, and especially in its imperialistic phase, war is inevitable."

Immediately after the capitalist world recovered from the post-war commotion and achieved provisional economic stabilization, a new wave of armaments came into being. All nations began developing feverishly those methods of warfare which the war had proved important, such as aviation, chemical warfare and tanks. The mechanization of armies and the modernization of fleets have been taking place universally. The

[1] J. Stalin: "Ob oppozitsii" ("On the Opposition"), articles and speeches, 1921–1927, State Publishing House, 1928, pp. 465–466.

attempt to keep these armaments at least within certain limits is frustrated by the action of the law which Lenin formulated as follows in his work "Imperialism as the Highest Stage of Capitalism:"

Financial capital and the trusts do not diminish but emphasize the difference in the tempo of growth between various parts of the world economy. But if the balance of forces has been broken, what can be used under a capitalistic system to bring about a settlement of the conflict except violence? [2]

And again:

Under capitalism no other basis is thinkable for the division of spheres of influence, interests, colonies, etc., except an estimate of the strength of the parties to the division, their general economic strength, their financial and military strength, and so on. But the strength of the parties to division changes unevenly, because an even development of separate enterprises, trusts, branches of industries, countries, is impossible under capitalism. Half a century ago Germany was a mere nonentity, if we compare her capitalistic strength with that of contemporary England; the same was true of Japan in comparison with Russia. Is it "thinkable" that one or two decades hence the relationship between the imperialist Powers should remain unaltered? Utterly unthinkable.

Under conditions actually prevailing in the capitalist world, therefore, the "inter-imperialistic" or "ultra-imperialistic" alliances—irrespective of the form these alliances might take, whether that of one imperialistic coalition against another imperialistic coalition, or that of a general alliance of all the imperialistic Powers—will necessarily be merely "breathing spaces" between wars.[3]

[2] Lenin: "Sobranie sochineni," Vol. XIX, p. 149.
[3] *Op. cit.*, Vol. XIX, pp. 167–168.

The opinions expressed by Lenin in 1916, in the midst of the World War, have been fully corroborated by post-war history. They explain why the capitalist world is incapable of obtaining any effective limitation in armaments and is therefore inescapably moving toward a new world war for a new re-distribution of the world.

Germany, having strengthened her industry with the help of American, English, Dutch and Swiss loans, and confronted with a shrinkage of the world market, cannot exist within the narrow limits assigned to her by the Treaty of Versailles. In seeking equality in armaments she is seeking the possibility for preparing a war for the revision of the Versailles peace.

Japan, who developed her industry first on the basis of an inhuman semi-feudal exploitation of the village population (which still continues), later with the help of billions of war profits, and who is half-strangled in the knot of surviving feudalism which, in an even stronger degree than the laws of imperialism, prevents the development of her domestic market—Japan, who understands that the United States is compelled by the entire course of its economic development to deepen and expand its struggle for economic influence in China—Japan, fearful that as a consequence of the industrialization of Siberia she will lose her monopolistic position as the only industrial country in the Far East—Japan tears up the Washington and the London agreements, occupies Manchuria, and gets ready to occupy

China before the economic domination of the United States has been fully established there. She raises the question of her hegemony over Asia. This objective has been openly proclaimed by Japan's Minister of War, General Araki.

Italy, "offended at Versailles," seeks a re-distribution of colonial lands in her favor.

The relations between the United States and England have suffered a fundamental change since the United States has risen to the position of being the first industrial power in the world and has claimed equality in the control of the seas.

The uneven development of post-war capitalism has created a situation in which all the imperialistic Powers will seek to re-distribute the world in accordance with their own interests.

The Soviet Union is opposed to imperialism. It is opposed to an imperialistic war. It recognizes as equitable only one war, the war for the defense of socialism, the war of the enslaved peoples for their liberation. This point of view determines our attitude toward imperialism, as a system, and toward the consequences of its policy which find their expression in the preparation of a new war. It also dictates our attitude toward imperialistic alliances which evolve during the process of preparing a new war for the re-distribution of the world.

The Soviet Union takes no part in the struggle for the re-distribution of the world.

The words of Stalin at the Sixteenth Congress of the Communist Party of the Soviet Union—"We do not want a single bit of foreign land; but at the same time not an inch of our land shall ever be yielded to anyone else"—these words are the exact expression of the policy of the Soviet Union.

In the struggle for the new re-distribution of the world the Soviet Union does not share. Taking account of the solidarity of the workers of the whole world, it can take no part in the plundering of foreign lands. Moreover, it does not need foreign land to carry on the work of constructing socialism. This policy found expression in the Soviet attitude toward the struggle in Manchuria. Defending its economic interests in connection with the Chinese Eastern Railroad, the Soviet Union never accepted the partition of Manchuria into spheres of influence. It followed a similar policy in Persia, even though this rendered its relations with British imperialism somewhat more difficult. Non-participation in imperialistic alliances having for their purpose the plundering of foreign lands is the second leading principle of the foreign policy of the Soviet Union.

But the preparation of an imperialistic war is a fact, the existence of imperialistic alliances is a fact, and the Soviet Union cannot limit itself to a mere expression of its negative attitude toward the objects of imperialism and toward imperialistic alliances. The Soviet Union must do everything to protect itself against the attack of the capitalist Powers who intend to conquer a portion of the Soviet territory or to overthrow the political framework of the socialist state.

The peace policy of the Soviet manifests itself not only in the struggle for disarmament, the struggle for the maximum reduction in armaments, but also in non-aggression pacts. In any given concrete case such a pact means a guarantee of Soviet neutrality in conflicts which may arise among the capitalist nations, conceded in exchange for the undertaking by the latter to refrain from attacking the Soviet Union or intervening in its domestic affairs. There is nothing surprising, therefore, in the fact that the first non-aggression pact concluded by the Soviet Union was with Turkey, for friendly relations between the two countries had developed from the early help offered by the Soviet Union to Turkey in her struggle for independence. Nor is it surprising that the next state with which the Soviet Union entered into a pact equivalent to a non-aggression pact was Germany (April 24, 1926). In its fight against the Treaty of Versailles, Germany tried to establish friendly relations with the Soviet Union as the only Great Power which opposed the enslavement of one nation by another. The non-aggression pacts with Afghanistan, in 1926, and with Persia, in 1929, were results of the policy of the Soviet Union which bases its relations with the Eastern peoples on the idea of equality and respect for their national independence.

It is not mere chance that for many years all attempts to conclude similar non-aggression pacts with the western neighbors of the Soviet Union remained fruitless. Those western neighbors for a long time participated openly or indirectly in the alignment of the victorious imperialistic Powers which had not given up the idea of intervention against the Soviets. Only experience—the experience which proved to these western neighbors of the Soviet Union that this policy not only does not protect their independence but might even weaken their position at the same time that they have to face the growing demand for the restoration of German imperialism—it was this experience only which developed their tendency toward peace with the Soviet Union and led to the conclusion of the non-aggression pacts between the Soviet Union, Poland, Latvia, Esthonia and Finland. A similar change in the general situation on the continent, Germany's growing desire to revise the conditions imposed upon her by the Treaty of Versailles—peacefully if possible, forcibly if necessary—proved to be one of the factors which induced France to enter into a non-aggression pact with the Soviet Union. Italy has been among the first to resume normal relations with the Soviet Union. It was her desire to strengthen her position with reference to France which influenced her to join the Soviet Union not only in a non-aggression pact but also in a pact of friendship. Soviet attempts to conclude a similar pact with Japan have up to the present time produced no positive results; this seems merely to indicate the existence in Japan of very strong tendencies to preserve complete freedom of action in case of conflict with the Soviet Union.

The Soviet Union is confronted both in Europe and the Far East with hostile camps which are preparing war against one another. It holds toward them a position of neutrality, and endeavors to guarantee its own peace by a policy of non-interference in their affairs and by entering into mutual obligations of non-aggression with all sides. These obligations have been stated concretely and precisely in the pact containing the definition of the aggressor. The Soviet Government has definitely undertaken not to move its armed forces by land, sea or air across the frontiers of states which have assumed similar obligations, and also not to intervene directly or indirectly in their domestic affairs. All this indicates to the world that the policy of peace and neutrality on which the Soviet Union has embarked is not a mere diplomatic gesture, but a concrete political obligation the earnestness of which should be beyond question.

The Soviet Union enters into pacts of non-aggression with any country which is willing to sign such a pact, that is to say it is ready to enter into non-aggression pacts with countries which may eventually be at war. It therefore must take into consideration that while its pledge of peace and neutrality strengthens one of the belligerent countries they may be disadvantageous to the other side, which in consequence may attempt to repudiate its non-aggression pact, violate its obligations, and attack the Soviet Union. Besides, of course, any action is possible on the part of the Powers which have refused to sign non-aggression pacts. It goes without saying that the Soviet Union's reply to any attack on it would be military action fully commensurate with the statement of Stalin that "not an inch of our land shall ever be yielded to anyone else." But then a situation might arise when the Soviet Union would carry on action parallel with the enemy of its own enemy, or would even coöperate with him in a joint action. The policy to follow in such an eventuality was foreseen by Lenin during the discussion of the Brest-Litovsk peace negotiations. Under quite different conditions, for then the Soviet Union was weak militarily, Lenin outlined the fundamental solution of the problem. This solution remains today one of the guiding principles of Soviet policy. "From the moment of the victory of socialist construction in one of the countries, the question must be settled not from the point of view of the desirability of this or that imperialism, but exclusively from the point of view of the best conditions for the development and strengthening of socialist revolution, which has already begun," wrote Lenin in his thesis on the conclusion of a separate peace, on January 7, 1918.[4]

In his article "O chesotke" ("About the Rash"), of

[4] *Op. cit.*, Vol. XXII, p. 195.

February 22 of the same year, Lenin, criticizing those who objected as a matter of principle to the conclusion of an agreement with the Allies against German imperialism, wrote as follows:

If Kerensky, representative of the dominating class of the bourgeoisie, that is of the exploiters, enters into an agreement with the Anglo-French exploiters under which he obtains arms and potatoes, but conceals from the people other agreements which promise (in case of success) to one robber Armenia, Galicia, Constantinople, to the other Baghdad, Syria, and so on —then is it difficult to understand that the transaction is a dishonest, disgusting and revolting one from the point of view of both Kerensky and his friends? No. It is not difficult to understand. Any peasant will understand it, even the most backward and illiterate one.

But what if the representative of the exploited class, of those who suffer, after that class has overthrown the exploiters and has published and annulled all secret and grasping agreements, is the object of a treacherous attack by the German imperialists? Is he to be condemned for dealing with the Anglo-French robbers, for accepting their arms and potatoes in exchange for timber and so on? Should such an agreement be called dishonest, shameful, unclean?[5]

By giving a positive answer to the question of the feasibility of an agreement between the Soviet Union and an imperialistic Power which, for the sake of its own imperialistic interests, was willing to help the Soviet Union in its struggle against other attacking imperialistic Powers, Lenin at the same time answered the question as to the possible expansion of the policy of

[5] *Op. cit.*, Vol. XXII, p. 273.

the Soviet Union beyond the stage of neutrality in case of a struggle between the imperialistic Powers.

The Soviet Union does not close the door to the possibility of striking a deal with imperialistic Powers which are waging a struggle against other imperialistic Powers, if the latter attack the Soviet Union; but in entering into such an agreement the Soviet Union would not accept any responsibility for the specific purposes pursued by the imperialistic Powers parties to the agreement. Never and under no conditions would it participate in the plundering of other nations, because participation in such a plunder would be contrary to the international solidarity of the workers. But against an attacking imperialism, agreement is permissible with any opponent in order to defeat an enemy invading Soviet territory.

I think I have named the fundamental principles of Soviet foreign policy and have explained their interdependence. They are all derived from the basic fact that imperialism is unable to solve the great problems which mankind has to face today. A new imperialistic war will not solve them. It will lead to an immense destruction of productive forces, to unexampled sufferings among the masses of the people, and will achieve nothing except a new re-shuffling of the possessions of the capitalist world.

The Soviet Union is an enemy of imperialistic wars which arise from the fact that capitalism is no longer in a position to develop the productive forces of the human race, but that it is still capable of attempting to seize a piece of land which is being reserved for the exploitation of a given national bourgeoisie. That is how the world is pushed toward immense new upheavals. We are therefore certain that the masses, thrust into the turmoil of new wars, will seek a way out along the same road that was followed by the Soviet proletariat in 1917.

The object of the Soviet Government is to save the soil of the first proletariat state from the criminal folly of a new war. To this end the Soviet Union has struggled with the greatest determination and consistency. The defense of peace and of the neutrality of the Soviet Union against all attempts to drag it into the whirlwind of a world war is the central problem of Soviet foreign policy.

The Soviet Union follows the policy of peace because peace is the best condition for building up a socialist society. Fighting for the maintenance of peace, accepting obligations of neutrality toward the struggling camps of the imperialists, the Soviet Union has at the same time raised the military preparedness of the country to a level which answers the demands of national defense and the requirements of modern warfare. Its neutrality is a positive factor which the imperialistic Powers which have not yet lost the sense of realities will not fail to appreciate. Those of them which are unable to realize the importance of Soviet neutrality or are forced by the insoluble difficulties of their own position to risk an adventurous war against that huge country, with its dozens of millions of men united by a common desire for peace, a desire for peaceful creative work—to those Powers will be given the proofs that the generation which laid down the foundations of socialism is also capable of defending them with iron energy. And we are convinced that, irrespective of what might be the course of the war and who might be responsible for its origins, the only victor that would emerge from it would be the Soviet Union leading the workers of the whole world; for it alone has a banner which, in case of a war, can become the banner of the masses of the entire world.

CHAPTER VII

THE UNITED STATES
By John W. Davis

AN ATTEMPT to state the permanent bases of any nation's foreign policy opens a range for discussion too broad for the compass of a single essay. History, tradition, political structure, geographical location, commercial interests, all these, to say nothing of the ambitions of statesmen and the exigencies of the moment, go to the making of a foreign policy. Some of these factors are fixed and stable. Others must change with the changing times. Rarely is there entire consistency in the pursuit of the policies to which these factors give rise. It is only in the most abstract sense therefore that any policy or the bases on which it rests can be called permanent. Yet it is possible, with the aid of history, to give a hurried summary of certain ideals and purposes which seem to have run with reasonable persistence throughout the course of American diplomacy and which cannot be ignored in predicting its future direction.

Of these, the first in point of time, if not in point of importance, is the wish to abstain as far as possible from any participation in foreign questions in general and European questions in particular. The roots of this feeling go deep into the American past. It has as its background the world situation at the time the United States of America came into being. The instruments employed by European monarchs in the midst of their quarrels and jealousies to advance their several interests, the alliances and counter-alliances, the balances of power, the armaments and counter-armaments, the treaties open and secret, were stigmatized *en bloc* by the American colonists as the European system. Looking at the turmoil it had bred and the burdens it imposed, they set up after the Revolutionary War a government republican in character based upon ideas of human equality, personal liberty and popular sovereignty, which, whether original or borrowed, new or old, they were pleased to call American. They asked nothing more of the world at large than a chance to develop these ideas undisturbed. Between them and the turbulent shores of Europe rolled the broad Atlantic. Their homeland was an unpeopled continent of vast natural resources. And the same self-reliance which had brought them and their fathers across the waters made them confident of their power, if only they were let alone, to realize the great things the future held in store.

In such surroundings it was a priceless advantage to be aloof and neutral in a world that was torn by the contemplation of present and future wars. John Adams spoke for himself and his countrymen in the conversation he reports between himself and Richard Oswald in 1782: " 'You are afraid,' says Mr. Oswald today, 'of being made tools of the Powers of Europe.' 'Indeed I am,' said I. 'What Powers?' said he. 'All of them,' said I. 'It is obvious that all the Powers of Europe will be continually manœuvring with us to work us into their real or imaginary balances of power. They will all wish to make us a make-weight candle when they are weighing out their pounds.' "

There was no "philosophical tranquillity," as Baron von Nolcken, the Swedish Minister of St. James's, suggested to Adams in their long-distance watching of "European throat-cutting;" only a feeling that it was none of their business and that it would be fatal to the survival of the new-born nation if it took part in the mêlée.

This attitude, so easily understood, was erected into a dogma by Washington with his warning in the Farewell Address against implicating ourselves with Europe "by artificial ties in the ordinary vicissitudes of her politics or the ordinary combinations or collisions of her friendships or enmities;" and confirmed by Jefferson in his first inaugural declaring for "commerce and honest friendship with all nations—entangling alliances with none."

Tuned as these words were to the times and circumstances in which they were uttered, their effect upon the subsequent conduct of America has been continuous. Their weight cannot be exaggerated. They have been echoed in substance, if not in terms, by statesmen of every generation. They have been repeated and re-repeated from the platform and in the press until they have become clothed in the minds of most Americans with the dignity of axioms. When the fight over the ratification of the Treaty of Versailles and the Covenant of the League of Nations was on, they furnished the stock argument to those who opposed the Covenant; and it was only by appealing to their high authority that public sentiment, at one time overwhelmingly in favor of the League, could be reconciled to its rejection.

President Wilson himself did not challenge the general doctrine. He said: "I shall never myself consent to any entangling alliance, but I would gladly assent to a disentangling alliance—an alliance which would disentangle the peoples of the world from those combinations in which they seek their own separate and private interest and unite the people of the world to preserve the peace of the world upon a basis of common right and justice. There is liberty there, not limitation. There is freedom, not entanglement." He denied, and those who thought and still think with him denied, that there is anything in this of abandonment or desertion of the teachings of Washington and Jefferson. Indeed, it may safely be assumed that those great men would have been the last to claim perpetual authority for their advice.

The views expressed by John Quincy Adams as early

as the year 1826 do better justice to their memory. In his message to Congress announcing his intention to enter the conference with the other American republics at Panama he said that he "could not overlook the reflection that the counsel of Washington in that instance, like all the counsels of wisdom, was founded upon the circumstances in which our country and the world around us were situated at the time when it was given," and comparing "our situation and the circumstances of that time with the present day" he held that his acceptance of the invitation did not conflict with the counsel or policy of Washington. Political isolation in the strict and absolute sense was never the doctrine of Washington or Jefferson, nevertheless their warnings against permanent alliances and participation in matters not directly related to the welfare of the United States have lost little of their potency with the passage of the years.

An obvious corollary of this same teaching was the doctrine of non-intervention in the internal affairs of other nations. After proclaiming the right to set up a government of her own devising, and to pursue her course without molestation from abroad, America could do no less than concede to other nations the same rights she claimed for herself. Whether their form of government was despotic or liberal, regular or revolutionary, their domestic politics peaceful or turbulent, was to be none of her affair. It was not unnatural that the adoption of institutions similar to her own and founded on like political philosophy should from time to time arouse her sympathetic interest; it was inevitable that when her citizens began to push abroad she should invoke for them that measure of protection to which they were entitled by the law of nations; but non-intervention on her part in the domestic affairs of other nations was to be a fixed canon of conduct to be departed from only on the gravest occasion. As Secretary Seward observed in 1863: "Our policy of non-intervention, straight, absolute and peculiar as it may seem to other nations, has thus become a traditional one which could not be abandoned without the most urgent occasion, amounting to a manifest necessity." And again: "The United States leave to the government and people of every foreign state the exclusive settlement of their own affairs and the exclusive employment of their own institutions."

That a nation thus dedicated to the policies of political isolation and non-intervention should imagine itself a permanent neutral in any war between other Powers was entirely logical, even though events from time to time have falsified the logic, as events so often do. The strain upon this purposeful neutrality came promptly during the wars of the Napoleonic era. It reached the breaking point in the War of 1812 and a century later in 1917. Yet it cannot be denied that the instinctive reaction on the part of America to any foreign outbreak has been one of neutrality, followed by the renewed assertion of the rights of neutral commerce in non-contraband goods, or, to use the later nomenclature, the "freedom of the seas." Every war of the last century and a half has provoked diplomatic interchanges on the subject, in which, not always with entire consistency, the prevalent American contention has been that blockades to be respected must be effective; that only those articles are to be treated as contraband which are adapted for belligerent uses; and that the flag of a neutral nation must protect both the vessel and its cargo. Shaken as the principles of neutrality were by the events of the Great War, and dim as the hope may be for the preservation of neutrality in future wars, it must be accepted that American thought on the subject is still dominated by the ancient tradition.

With the delivery of President Monroe's message to Congress in 1823, the Monroe Doctrine came to its permanent place in American history. "The occasion," said he, "has been judged proper for asserting, as a principle in which the rights and interests of the United States are involved, that the American continents, by the free and independent condition which they have assumed and maintain, are not henceforth to be considered as subjects for future colonization by any European Powers. . . . We owe it, therefore, to candor, and to the amicable relations existing between the United States and those Powers, to declare that we should consider any attempt on their part to extend their system to any portion of this hemisphere as dangerous to our peace and safety."

It is worth while to quote the familiar words of this message because of the gloss that has so often been put upon them by orators and statesmen in the century that has followed their delivery. It is worth while also to notice that the sole reason put forward for the declaration was the peace and safety of the United States itself and not the protection of the newly formed South American Republics. There was in the declaration no assertion of overlordship or of hegemony in the Western Hemisphere, and least of all of a purpose to control or regulate the domestic affairs of our American neighbors. The creation of the Holy Alliance furnished the occasion, and national tranquillity supplied the motive, but there was no pretense of a general protectorate over other American states. As Secretary Olney defined it in his Venezuelan Boundary despatch: "The rule in question has but a single purpose and object. It is that no European Power or combination of European Powers shall forcibly deprive an American state of the right and power of self-government and of shaping for itself its own political fortunes and destinies." His bellicose sentence that, "Today the United States is practically sovereign on this continent, and its fiat is law upon the subjects to which it confines its interposition," could certainly not have been intended by its distinguished author as either an interpretation or an attempted enlargement of the Monroe Doctrine. In the calmer and less controversial atmosphere of today it would hardly be repeated lest it might be regarded as rodomontade. True, the Monroe Doctrine, as Americans understand it, has come with the passage of time to apply to all non-American Powers rather than to those of Europe alone, and to acquisitions of territory by the transfer of dominion and sovereignty as well as by colonization; but such further expansions as are to be found in the rhetoric of spread-eagle orators have no foundation either in tradition or in fact. The idea that the Monroe Doctrine is an all-embracing synopsis and epitome of our relations with our Latin American neighbors is a wholly erroneous conception.

The policies to which I have so far alluded, with the possible exception of those relating to neutral commerce, have a negative quality suitable to a nation set upon living an indoor life of oriental seclusion. Jefferson's ambition, indeed, was to see the United States a nation of self-supporting husbandmen. The national temper, however, was not adapted to such a future, and even in Jefferson's own day his countrymen were crowding into commerce and flocking to the open sea. Some were traders in time of peace engaged in nibbling into England's carrying trade, others were blockade runners in the Napoleonic wars, roving the seven seas. Under the spur of commercial ambition, American shipping throve mightily. In the early part of the nineteenth century the American clipper ships not only met the mariners of England in successful competition, but practically monopolized for a time the transport to England herself of China tea. There was an immediate need, therefore, for a positive foreign policy fixing the terms on which the new nation was to live in the trading world. The nations were still under the spell of the doctrines of "mercantilism" and trade restrictions, prohibitions and discriminations were wellnigh universal. Indeed, there was hardly a port in the Western Hemisphere outside their own country in which American vessels could lawfully trade.

To break these shackles was the first task of American diplomacy. The objective was announced in the preamble to the Treaty of 1778 with France in these words: "By taking for the basis of their agreement the most perfect equality and reciprocity, and by carefully avoiding all those burdensome preferences which are usually sources of debate, embarrassment and discontent; by leaving also each party at liberty to make respecting commerce and navigation those interior regulations which it shall find most convenient to itself; and by finding the advantage of commerce solely upon reciprocal utility and the just rules of free intercourse; reserving withal to each party the liberty of admitting at its pleasure other nations to a participation of the same advantages." This was, as John Quincy Adams called it, "The corner stone for all our subsequent transactions of intercourse with foreign nations."

So step by step, and with infinite labor, the ports of the colonies, first of Great Britain and then of Spain, were opened to American vessels upon reciprocal terms. One by one discriminating duties were removed and most-favored-nation treaties were negotiated with all the principal trading Powers of the world. The policy of reciprocity was deliberately adopted and steadily pursued; reciprocity in the sense of equal and impartial trade and not as the word has come to mean in its later usage—mutual or equivalent reductions of duties and imposts—the latter "a policy," as John Bassett Moore has wittily said, "recommended by free traders as an escape from protection and by protectionists as an escape from free trade, but distrusted by both and supported by neither."

It was left to John Hay in his negotiations in 1899 for the open door in China to secure the most dramatic of the later triumphs of this policy. Confronted by the impending partition of the territory and trade of China among foreign Powers, instead of engaging in the general scramble he chose a more effective course. Starting with the same English sympathy which had been shown by Canning when the Monroe Doctrine was promulgated, he secured in turn the assent of France, Germany, Russia, Italy and Japan to the principle of equal and impartial trade for the commerce of all nations in Chinese ports and spheres of influence. As a work of peace it was an achievement of the first magnitude. It came to further fruition at the Washington Conference of 1922, when the nine Powers there represented formally agreed to use their influence for the purpose of effectually establishing and maintaining the principle of equal opportunity for the commerce and industry of all nations throughout the territory of China.

I pass to another subject. In his inaugural address of March 4, 1897, President McKinley made bold to declare that arbitration as the true method of settling international questions "has been recognized as *the* leading feature of our foreign policy throughout our entire national history." Note the use of the definite article. The statement is hardly an exaggeration, notwithstanding the fact that the nation of which it was spoken has fought in the course of its history two civil and four foreign wars, without counting the innumerable conflicts waged with the Indian tribes. Such was the aggregate duration of these major wars that it may be said without overstatement that America has devoted at least one day out of every eight of its national life to the making of war; the remaining seven have been spent in paying the bills. In spite of a genuine passion for peace, therefore, the United States can hardly be called a pacifist nation. Yet, with unhappy stumblings by the way, it has from the making of the Jay Treaty to this date endeavored to follow the road of arbitrament rather than of conflict. It has been a party itself to over 85 arbitrations with some 25 countries; and by precept and example it has commended the practice of arbitration to mankind. It stands today definitely committed, so far as the Executive and its past professions can commit it, to the support and maintenance of the Permanent Court of

International Justice; and if it has forfeited anything of its former glory as a champion of international arbitration, the loss must be charged to the account of Senatorial jealousy of Senatorial prerogative and Senatorial difficulty in making up two-thirds of the Senatorial mind.

If in the course of this brief outline I have leaned heavily on the sayings of men of earlier days, it is not without reason. With all their spirit of enterprise and innovation, the American people are at heart traditionalists. In matters of government they are prone to take the beaten paths. And in spite of their sense of human equality they are likewise hero-worshippers. They are accustomed, moreover, to written formulæ in their government, their politics, even in their business. An argument buttressed by quotation from a national hero has its battle half won from the start. Whatever the demand for a shift in thought may be, it is useless to disguise the fact that they find it easier to inquire what Washington, for instance, may have said, than to consider what wisdom like Washington's would say today.

A general survey of American foreign relations could not conclude without adverting to other important topics. Such, for instance, are the disarmament of the Canadian border; the cultivation of friendship with our neighbors to the south under the name of Pan-Americanism; the protection of the Panama Canal and the policing of the Caribbean; the problems of the

Pacific and the consultative pact of Washington; and, latterly, naval disarmament and naval parity with Great Britain. These and many similar matters could not be ignored by the diplomatic historian, but the aim of this essay is far less ambitious. The effort here, I repeat, is to discover, with the aid of history, those ideas which run with such persistence throughout our foreign policy as to indicate their permanent fixation in the national mind; political isolation, non-intervention, neutrality, the Monroe Doctrine, the open door, arbitration—these threads seem to run all through the warp and woof of our national weaving. It is quite easy for the critic to show that they have been broken from time to time. They disappear from the pattern here and reappear later there—consistency is no more a virtue of nations than of men—yet without them there would be little to give coherence and unity to the design.

Is there any common bond between these policies themselves, any consistent idea which has inspired them, any common stuff out of which they have been spun? I think there can be no doubt of it. Stated in the simplest terms, the dominating desire on the part of the American people as expressed in their foreign policy has been to be free to mind their own business without interference and to permit others to do the same. This of itself is not a policy, but it is the motive by which policies have been inspired. Nor must it be supposed that there is anything unique or singular in this attitude. The people of every nation cherish the wish to work out their own destiny after their own fashion, and for this reason the mainspring of national action is always self-interest. It could not properly be otherwise. Those who, by reason of their official position, have the power to frame and carry out the foreign policies of their country are not proprietors but trustees of the power they hold. They dare not use this power to satisfy mere personal ambition or to advance their personal fortunes. They are not even free to spend it in works of unrequited charity, no matter how noble. True to their trust, they must at all points consider first and always the welfare and safety of the people they are called to serve. Self-interest, albeit the enlightened self-interest, of the nation is to be their constant guide.

This desire to be let alone is but the same idea which is embodied in the word "security," an expression used and interpreted by every people in the light of their own peculiar circumstances. To some it brings to mind the threatened boundaries between themselves and hostile Powers; to some the long lines of ocean communication on which their very lives depend; while still others look abroad to their colonial possessions and fear for the links that bind them to the mother country. Fortunately for America, she hears the march of no hostile armies along her frontiers; no blockade of her coasts can bring famine to her firesides; and while she must defend the outposts she possesses, neither the genius of her institutions nor her past experience fosters in her any ambition to play the rôle of a colonizing Power. Indeed, taking her venture in the Philippines as an example, it would be fair to say that, while opinions differ widely as to her present and future responsibilities there, most Americans in their heart of hearts regard the original retention of the islands as a sorry blunder and devoutly wish that Dewey, after he had destroyed the Spanish fleet in Manila Bay, had weighed his anchors and made for the open sea.

But the fact that America is not oppressed by considerations such as these does not make her foreign policy any the less a search for security than that of Powers not so fortunate. Time, of course, has brought great changes since she first began to think in national terms. Her entire geography, for one thing, has altered; where she once looked out on one ocean, she now looks out on two. While she held at first but a fringe along the shoreline, she now spreads across a continent; and since the acquisition of Hawaii, Puerto Rico and the Philippines, and the building of the Panama Canal, her shadow falls far beyond the confines of the Union. As she has reached out to make contact with the world, the world with its steamships, aircraft, cables and radios has advanced to meet her, until distance no longer decides the relationship between herself and the rest of mankind. Commerce has altered quite as much as geography since the day when a colonial request for episcopal guidance was answered by the brusque remark, "Damn their souls, let them grow tobacco." And finance, by means of loans and fixed investments, has scattered all over the globe, not the imaginary funds of "international bankers," but the collective savings of the American people, in the hope that this seed in time will bring its harvest of profit and reward. Perhaps no nation in the world has seen greater changes in the same length of time.

In view of these facts it is clear that the statement that America wishes to be free to mind her own business is not an answer to a question but merely the introduction to a series of questions that must be answered if phrase-mongering is not to take the place of reasoning in her foreign policy. In the word "security" today are wrapped up many things which could not have been dreamed of a century ago. So long as the world obstinately refuses to become static and unchangeable, "never" is a dangerous word for governments or statesmen to employ. Policy must always be elastic enough to fit changed surroundings, for the change of surroundings does not wait on policy. "I do not control events," said Lincoln, "I am controlled by them." If the foreign policies that have guided America hitherto are no longer adequate to preserve her peace and insure her prosperity, it does not necessarily follow that they should be abandoned; but it does render it imperative that they should be supplemented by further policies consciously adapted to her present needs.

Quite obviously the day has gone by, if indeed it ever existed, when America could think of her interests and duties apart from those falling to her as a member of the community of nations. The march of science, the advance in the arts of communication, the interlocking activities of commerce and finance, her own expanding needs and desires have made that no longer possible. Recent events have served to drive the lesson home even to that presumptively ignorant but ubiquitous person, the man-in-the-street. The Great War has shown him over what vast distances the sound of a cannon shot will travel, and the subsequent depression joined the American wheat farmer and the British coal miner in a common misery. The question is no longer whether America will join the concert of the nations. By the decrees of Providence and the pressure of inexorable events she is already there beyond hope of escape, and is permitted to consider only the manner in which she shall bear herself in that relationship.

Judging the future by the past, it is extremely unlikely that she will ever throw off her fixed aversion to alliances for peace or war with special Powers. It seems in no way necessary and would probably be most unfortunate if she did. Yet since it is no longer possible for her to sit in calm seclusion, prudence and duty unite in dictating to her a thoroughgoing, ungrudging, and generous coöperation with the rest of the world in the organization and maintenance of peace; for peace and the liberty of action it insures are the things she most needs to work out her destiny. There is no dodging the stern fact that today American security, repose, prosperity—what you will—are dependent in chief measure on America's contribution to world security. For this contribution pious aspirations and benevolent phrases are pitiful substitutes, and pharisaic self-righteousness the least helpful substitute of all. If the organization and maintenance of peace by common action has its risks, they are as dust in the balance alongside the hideous certainties of modern war. Any foreign policy that falls short of the last effort to avert this peril can only be described as a thing limping and incomplete.

This is not, as some would have it, the dreaming of the idealist: it is realism of the most severe and practical sort. I go back again to Jefferson. On assuming the office of Secretary of State, he wrote to Lafayette: "I think with others that nations are to be governed with regard to their own interests, but I am convinced that it is their interests in the long run to be grateful, faithful to their engagements even in the worst of circumstances, and honorable and generous always."